Security Prices in a Competitive Market

Richard A. Brealey

SECURITY PRICES IN A
COMPETITIVE MARKET:

More about Risk and Return from Common Stocks

 The M.I.T. Press
Cambridge, Massachusetts, and London, England

Contents

Part II
UNUSUAL ACTIVITY AND THE STOCK PRICE

Part III
CONVERTIBLE SECURITIES

Preface

In recent years there has developed in the United States a widespread interest in the nature and causes of stock price movements. The increasing number of people with a training in both finance and statistics, the ready availability of computers, and the development of comprehensive financial data banks have contributed to the production of a large number of empirical studies of market behavior. Very little of this work has so far had any impact on the way investors go about their business. This is not altogether surprising in view of the newness of most of the research, but there are difficulties that will not be solved by the passage of time alone. One is that of access to the work. A large proportion of the material is never published, and, even when it is, the specific discipline of the author may lead it to appear in journals that are not ordinarily concerned with finance. In addition, the papers are often not addressed to the investor and require a familiarity with the techniques and language of the author's specialty.

The merits of this careful research are also in some danger of being obscured by a welter of nonsensical claims that have been made in the name of science. The new alchemy is no more promising than the old, for there is no primrose path to great wealth. The main potential value of quantitative financial research is that it can lead to a better understanding of the environment in which the investor works. This belief underlies the chapters that follow. They draw on a wide range of empirical research to provide in language familiar to the investor a description of certain features of the equity market as seen through the eyes of the statistician.

In the last few years a number of commentators have put forward the suggestion that equity investment is akin to a fair game. According to this view, the strong competition among participants causes public information to be rapidly impounded in the price of a stock, so that the investor can generally expect neither more nor less than a fair reward for the risks involved. Certain features of this theory were discussed in a companion volume,* which dealt principally with the relationship between risk and prospective return. The present book examines some other evidence of market efficiency. The first part is devoted to an analysis of investor reaction to corporate financial decisions. It considers the role of dividend policy and financial structure, of the possible benefits from mergers, and of the impact of stock splits and exchange listings. In the main, corporate decisions appear to affect the price of the stock only insofar as they produce or indicate a change in the substantive value of the enterprise. The second part discusses the manner

---

* Richard A. Brealey, *An Introduction to Risk and Return from Common Stocks.* Cambridge, Mass.: M.I.T. Press, 1969.

in which stock prices react to certain kinds of unusual activity, such as the sale of a very large block of stock or the accumulation of stock by a specific group of investors. A rich body of market folklore holds that these are valuable warning signals for the stockholder. However, the evidence of Part II suggests that the market is well able to recognize and discount the significance of these activities. The book's third part is concerned with the manner in which the market appraises more complex assets. In certain instances these securities seem to appeal to investors with unusual tastes or opportunities, but where this is not the case, they appear to be priced in accordance with the "fair game" theory.

Most of the specific issues in this book are simple and well defined. Yet despite all the tools of modern statistics, many of these questions are far from resolved. In a number of instances this is explained by the fact that the topic has received little attention, but frequently it is due to difficulties that are inherent in the subject.

One problem is recurrent. There are many interrelated factors that affect the price of a stock, and they are not easily identified or measured. Yet, if one does not take all the relevant variables into account, the answers may be very misleading. This problem may be illustrated with an example drawn from the field of medicine. Between 1948 and 1952 a now-famous survey was made of nearly 1500 lung-cancer patients throughout England and Wales and of an identical number of patients suffering from other diseases. The fact that a much larger proportion of the lung-cancer group admitted to smoking lent some credence to earlier suspicions that this habit is an important factor in the production of carcinoma of the lung. However, any such test is liable to the objection that there may exist a third factor that may both encourage smoking and induce cancer. The researchers in the present case sought to anticipate this contention first by matching the samples according to age, sex, and hospital and second by analyzing them according to such characteristics as residence and previous respiratory diseases. Nevertheless, despite the passage of twenty years and the evidence of several more large surveys, the controversy continues. The problem is twofold, for it is necessary not only to identify all the relevant factors but also to measure them accurately. For example, suppose that the only connection between smoking and lung cancer is that they are both induced by nervous tension. If this condition could not always be detected, any investigation would suggest that even among the more placid members of the community heavy smokers were more liable to cancer.

Many of the continuing controversies in the field of investment center on just such problems of identification and measurement, and much of this book is concerned with the ingenious attempts of researchers to circumvent them.

A large number of empirical studies are brought together in the following chapters. A list of these works is provided at the end of the book, and reference numbers are incorporated in the text. It should, however, be stressed that the interpretation placed upon the results is not necessarily that of the original author.

The reader is directed to B. G. Malkiel and J. Cragg, "Expectations and the Structure of Share Prices," *American Economic Review* 60 (September 1970): 601–617, for the published version of the paper listed as Reference 35. Since my Table 26 does not appear in the published version of the article by Lorie and Niederhoffer, I have listed the unpublished version as well (Reference 93).

Acknowledgments

My obligations are widespread. I am particularly indebted to Professor Robert Glauber, Harvard Business School, Professor Myron Scholes, Sloan School of Management, Massachusetts Institute of Technology, and Dr. Dean Paxson for comments on early versions of the manuscript. I have also benefited from the opportunity to discuss a number of topics with Professor James Lorie of the University of Chicago Graduate School of Business. Among those who have helped to supply me with material I am particularly grateful to Mr. Michael Hall of Phillips and Drew, London, Mr. John McNeel of the United States Trust Company, New York, Dr. Philip Brown, Department of Commerce, University of Western Australia, and Dr. Victor Niederhoffer, School of Business Administration, University of California, Berkeley.

The labor of typing the manuscript was borne by Miss Christine Chapman and my wife.

Part I
FINANCIAL POLICY AND THE STOCK PRICE

What is it that causes the market to value some stocks more highly than others? Most investors would probably agree that these differences are in large measure due to differences in the firms' earnings prospects, for stocks of companies whose earnings are expected to grow unusually fast customarily sell at a higher price relative to earnings than those of their less dynamic competitors. This is demonstrated in Figure 1. Here the price-earnings multiples of nearly 150 stocks have been plotted against one investor's view of the earnings prospects. The tendency for these points to cluster along an upward-slopping line

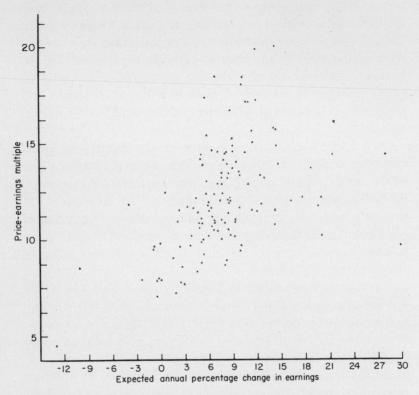

FIGURE I. Relation between price-earnings multiple and one investor's view of long-term earnings growth (courtesy of Phillips and Drew).

is testimony to the fact that a high multiple implies a belief that earnings will grow at an above-average rate.

On occasion the connection between the multiple and the long-term earnings prospects may be obscured by temporary incidents that seriously distort the company's current earning power. For this reason a clearer relation might emerge if long-term earnings prospects were plotted against the ratio of price to normalized earnings.

One analysis along these lines sought to measure market expectations by averaging the earnings predictions made by nine institutions for nearly 170 companies in each of the years 1961–1965.[35] Two of these institutions also contributed their assessment of the most recent level of earnings as adjusted for abnormal conditions. On the average, approximately two-thirds of the variation in the ratio of price to adjusted earnings could be explained in terms of differences in the anticipated earnings growth.

Such findings constitute strong evidence that the expected change in earnings exerts a notable influence on the market value of the stock, but one should be cautious of accepting too readily precise measurements of this influence. Not only might the market's appraisal of the outlook be very different from that of the chosen institutions, but the relation between the stock price and the expected rate of growth is likely to be more complex than this exercise assumed.

Suppose, however, that in Figure 1 the scatter about the upward-sloping line is not merely due to an incomplete description of the relation between price and prospective earnings. What other factors could cause two stocks with identical earnings prospects to sell at different prices? And what are the implications for a company that wishes to maximize the present price of its stock? These questions are considered in the chapters that follow.

Chapter 1 *Dividends and the Stock Price*

If in 1926 a tax-exempt investor had purchased an equal amount of all New York Stock Exchange equities, and if he had reinvested all subsequent dividends, he would have found that by the end of forty years his capital had multiplied thirty-five times.[51] If he had been improvident and squandered all his dividends on bacchanalian pleasures, the value of his portfolio would have increased by a factor of only six. This example is presented not as a warning against prodigality but to demonstrate that the cumulative effect of dividend receipts can be very large.

The return from an investment depends both on the income it produces and on the change in its capital value. Yet, because the latter component is more variable and difficult to predict, it can sometimes monopolize the investor's attention. This effect may be strengthened by the almost universal practice of exaggerating anticipated changes in price. Compared with the 4.6% per annum by which prices rose over the forty-year period, the yield of 2.7% was important. Compared with the appreciation that many claim to foresee from their favorite stocks, the yield dwindles into insignificance. When assessing a portfolio's performance, it is no less essential to consider the total return. Seriously misleading conclusions can result when funds with very different rates of dividend income are compared only in terms of their capital appreciation.

If two firms offer equally good prospects of growth in per-share earnings, the market should value more highly the company that can combine such a rate of expansion with a generous dividend payment. There is plenty of evidence that this is so. For example, the exercise described in the introduction to Part I was extended to consider the effect on the adjusted price-earnings multiple both of the prospective earnings growth and of the payout ratio.[35] After taking into account any difference in the expected rates of growth, the market appeared to place a higher value on companies whose growth was not likely to depend simply on large retentions.

This implies only that dividend yield and capital gain are both esteemed by investors. It does not indicate whether they are esteemed equally. Yet for a company that is faced with the problem of deciding on a suitable dividend policy this is an important question. If shareholders welcome a certain payout ratio for its own sake, a simple means is available for many companies to increase the price of their stock.

Before looking at the empirical evidence on the subject, it might be well to consider why investors should have any preferences of this nature. It is easiest initially to examine the problem in the context of a market where there is no taxation or cost involved in stock transactions or flotations. In such circumstances investors might be expected to be largely indifferent to the level of payout.[102] If a company's dividend distribution were insufficient to satisfy the investor's need for current income, he would have the option of selling a small proportion of his holding each year to offset the shortfall. If, on the other hand, the distribution were in excess of his requirements, he could reinvest the surplus in the company's stock. Similarly, in this idealized environment company operations would not be affected by the dividend decision. If retained earnings proved to be insufficient for the firm's investment program, they could be supplemented by a rights issue of stock. If they were excessive, they could be devoted to the repurchase of stock.

Even under these simplified conditions it is possible to envisage circumstances that might cause the investor to prefer companies with certain rates of payout. In the first place, it could be a nuisance to have to compensate for the effect of a dividend rate that did not match the need for current income. Second, there may be prejudices, however irrational, against the use of capital for purposes of income or even against the reinvestment of income. This can be particularly important in the case of institutions that are bound by trust deeds or government regulation to distinguish between capital and income or to limit their holdings to securities with established dividend records.

It is also sometimes argued that investors may prefer a high rate of payout because dividends are more certain than capital gains, the probable alternative.[60,90] This suggestion is unacceptable. It is not the dividend policy as such that affects the risk, but the fact that the payment reduces the proportion of the investor's assets in equities. If he reestablished his position in the stock by reinvesting the dividend, his risk would increase correspondingly.

Once the assumption of no transaction or flotation costs is removed, an additional reason emerges for the investor to be concerned with the rate of payout. From the company's viewpoint, rights issues may become an expensive alternative to retained earnings. For the investor, the reinvestment of excessive dividends or the sale of stock to augment an inadequate income is liable to involve appreciable commission charges. Such expenses can explain why different investors should prefer different dividend policies, but they can cause one type of stock to stand at a premium only if investors as a whole are receiving in dividends smaller or larger sums than they require. Although this is not impossible, it is difficult to believe that over the long term the average rate of disbursement differs markedly from the average desired rate.

The assumption of zero taxation may be more critical. The differential rates of tax on dividends and capital gains can be expected to favor low-payout stocks. In these circumstances the choice between the shareholder's reinvesting a part of his dividends and the company's distributing a lower proportion of earnings ceases to be a matter of no consequence. Even the investor with relatively high income requirements may be better off holding a low-payout stock and satisfying his demand for cash by selling small amounts of stock at regular intervals. For this reason, one might expect low-payout shares to sell at somewhat higher prices and to provide lower returns before tax.

It has been estimated that the marginal rate of tax on income for the individual shareholder was 42% in 1955 and 35% in 1965.[72] Because dividend receipts are not always reported to the Internal Revenue Service, these figures are more likely than not to be an overstatement. In addition, since many institutions enjoy a privileged tax status, the marginal rate for investors as a whole must be lower still. Some further evidence on the question is provided by the yield spreads between corporate and tax-exempt bonds. These can be explained by assuming an investor tax bracket of 20%–25%.[55] As the bond market is dominated more by the institutional investor, one might judge that the marginal rate of tax on income for the average stockholder is in the region of 25%–30%. The comparable figure for capital gains is less easily assessed. One estimate has suggested that approximately 80% of capital gains are unrealized or offset by losses and therefore escape taxation.[7] Since the average rate of tax on long-term gains that do not escape is in the region of 20% for individuals,[91] it is clear that the total payment of capital-gains tax constitutes only a very small proportion of the increase in capital values.

If investors are strongly influenced by the lower rates of tax on capital gains, one would expect to find that low-payout stocks are particularly favored by individuals with high marginal rates of tax. Table 1 shows that high-income groups have

TABLE 1. *Dividends in 1959 as a Percentage of Realized Long-Term Capital Gains by Income Class*

Adjusted Gross Income	Dividends as Percentage of Net Long-Term Capital Gains
Under $10,000	376%
$10,000–$50,000	223
$50,000–$100,000	186
$100,000–$200,000	144
$200,000–$500,000	85
$500,000–$1,000,000	61
$1,000,000 or more	70
All incomes	186%

Source: After Brittain.[27] Copyright © 1966 by The Brookings Institution. Adapted by permission.

tended to receive an unusually large proportion of their return in the form of realized capital gains. Although this is consistent with the view that they are seeking to minimize their tax burden, it may be that high-income groups are simply more active traders. Additional evidence suggests that in low-payout companies ownership is concentrated in fewer hands.[34,36] This again may indicate that such stocks are preferred by wealthy individuals. However, a more detailed examination of stock ownership in Wisconsin uncovered no significant tendency for high-income groups to prefer low-payout stocks.[5]

Evidence of a different character was obtained by two surveys of investor aims. The results of the first, which was conducted in 1949, are shown in Table 2.[29] The relative importance

TABLE 2. *Investment Objectives of a Sample of 736 Active Investors Interviewed in 1949*

Income Class (thousands of $)	Investment Objectives				
	Capital Preservation	Security and Income	Income	Income and Capital Appreciation	Capital Appreciation
Under 7.5	4%	42%	26%	20%	8%
7.5–12.5	5	41	17	28	9
12.5–25	8	32	20	31	9
25–50	6	24	19	42	9
50–100	20	18	13	33	16
Over 100	12	7	9	46	26

Source: After Butters, Thompson, and Bollinger.[29]

attached to income and capital gains varied consistently with income groups. Similarly, in a later survey, conducted by Merrill Lynch, not only did a majority of the respondents place capital appreciation at the head of their list of objectives, but the emphasis placed on it varied according to their income.

Some further indication of the relative value that investors place on dividends may be procured by looking at what happens to stock prices on ex-dividend dates. This is to some extent determined by the New York Stock Exchange regulation that on such occasions the specialist should reduce all open bids and all stop-sell orders by the gross value of the dividend. Therefore any tendency for the price to decline by less than this amount would reinforce the notion that stockholders' actions are affected by the higher rates of tax on income. There have been a number of studies of this subject, and the results are summarized in Table 3. The bulk of the evidence points to the

TABLE 3. *Price Decline on Ex-Dividend Dates and Implied Tax Brackets*

Dates	No. of Observations	Price Measured from Close to:	Average Decline as Percentage of Dividend	Implied Tax Bracket
1951–1955[a]	2500	Opening	81%	32%
1966–1967[b]	4148	Close	79	35
1949–1950[c]	199	Opening	92	13
1953[c]	200	Opening	85	30
1948–1959[d]	43	Close	96	7

[a] Source: After Readett.[118]
[b] Source: After Elton and Gruber.[45]
[c] Source: After Campbell and Beranek.[30]
[d] Source: After Durand and May.[43]

fact that on the ex-dividend date the price falls by approximately 85% of the gross value of the dividend. It is worth giving up a dollar of dividends for 85 cents of long-term capital gain only if the investor is subject to a marginal rate on income in the region of 30%.

This analysis can be taken one step further by looking at the way in which behavior on ex-dividend dates varies according to the firm's payout rate.[45] This has been done in Table 4. Where the companies distribute a small proportion of earnings, the price decline on the ex-dividend day constitutes a lesser proportion of the dividend, which suggests that these stocks are being bought mainly by investors in high tax brackets. Once again it appears that investors are aware of the slight tax advantage to low-payout stocks.

TABLE 4. *Price Decline on Ex-Dividend Dates and Implied Tax Brackets of 4148 Stocks Grouped According to Payout Ratio*

Group	Average Payout Ratio	Average Decline as Percentage of Dividend	Implied Tax Bracket
1	20%	68%	49%
2	32	67	49
3	37	76	39
4	41	73	43
5	45	74	41
6	49	68	48
7	53	102	0
8	59	90	19
9	67	93	8
10	104	90	22

Source: After Elton and Gruber.[45]

This indirect evidence points in the opposite direction to the teachings of most investment texts. Graham and Dodd, for example, state that

the considered and continuous verdict of the stock market is overwhelmingly in favor of liberal dividends as against niggardly ones. The common stock investor and the security analyst must take this judgment into account in the valuation of stocks for purchase. It is now becoming standard practice to evaluate common stock by applying one multiplier to that portion of the earnings paid out in dividends and a much smaller multiplier to the undistributed balance.[62]

Another author has recommended a law enforcing full distribution of earnings on the grounds that it "would almost certainly double or treble (within a short period) the market value of equities." [125] It is an Elysian prospect.

When one begins to look at the price of stocks with different rates of distribution, it is possible to see how this view has arisen. For example, Table 5 shows the price-earnings ratios

TABLE 5. *Relation between Dividend Policy and Market Valuation of 138 Stocks*

Payout (%)	Average Price-Earnings Ratio				
	1945	1946	1947	1948	1949
0– 20	18.8	6.2	5.6	3.7	7.5
20– 40	13.6	9.1	7.1	5.1	6.4
40– 60	16.9	12.0	8.7	7.0	8.3
60– 80	22.0	14.7	11.9	10.8	10.5
80–100	23.5	18.2	15.5	11.6	11.5
>100	38.8	31.7	14.9	—	17.2

Source: After Robinson.[121]

of 138 stocks that have been classified according to the size of their payout ratio.[121] In each year there was a clear tendency for the market to value more highly companies that distributed a substantial proportion of their earnings. Numerous studies have extended this approach. They have embraced both American and British securities. Sometimes the data have been drawn from one industry, sometimes the sample has been general. Natural and logarithmic relations have been assumed. The conclusions have been unanimous. A dollar of dividends was worth anything up to four times as much as a dollar of retained earnings.

Unfortunately, the analysis involves several biases. For instance, suppose that a company that customarily distributed half of its earnings suffered a prolonged labor dispute that caused its profits to dwindle almost to nothing. As long as the setback was thought to be short lived, the company would probably not reduce the dividend, so that the full effect of the earnings decline would be absorbed by retentions. In such circumstances the stock price would also react less than earnings. Indeed, the maintenance of the dividend might well be interpreted by the market as a demonstration of management's confidence in an earnings recovery. Thus the company's misfortune leads both to a high rate of payout and to a high earnings multiple, but it would be wrong to infer from this association that the market is indifferent to changes in retained earnings. Indeed, the kind of phenomenon observed in Table 5 will always occur if both the dividend and the stock price are determined in the light of more than just the one year's earnings. It will be particularly marked if investors read into the company's dividend decision some indication of future prospects.

A related source of error in these analyses could result from the omission of other factors that may affect both the firm's dividend policy and the market valuation. For example, companies that are highly leveraged or subject to considerable variations in their cash flow appear to adopt a relatively conservative attitude toward dividends.[57] These risks will affect not only the company's thinking but also that of the market, so that the stock is likely to sell at a below-average multiple. Again the result is an association between the price of the stock and the payout ratio, but it does not occur because the market prefers dividend yield to capital appreciation.

In view of these difficulties, it may be worth trying a somewhat different approach. If investors do not distinguish between current income and capital gains, they would be quite content as long as the sum of the dividend yield and the prospective earnings growth came up to requirements. If, however, they prefer current income, they would weight earnings growth less heavily in determining whether the return was sufficient. This can be stated more formally as

Required return = dividend yield + b × expected earnings growth.

If investors do not care about the firm's distribution policy, b in this equation should have a value of 1. On the other hand, if earnings growth carries less weight with the investor, b should be less than 1. It may also be necessary to allow for the possibility that some stocks may involve above-average risks, for in such instances the market will demand to be compensated by higher returns. The equation can, therefore, be expanded to read

Required return = required return from average stock + c × unusual risks = dividend yield + b × expected earnings growth.

Finally, the items in the equation can be rearranged, so that

Dividend yield = $a - b$ × expected earnings growth + c × unusual risks,

where a denotes the required rate of return from the average stock. The advantage to formulating the problem in this somewhat involved manner is that it is possible to make reasonable estimates of each item, particularly if the selection of issues is limited to a homogeneous group such as utility stocks. Since the profitability of a utility is regulated, investors must look to plowback as the main source of earnings growth; consequently, the expected earnings growth can be assumed to be equal to the percentage addition that retentions would make to the equity base if earnings were on trend. The measurement of risk is not an easy matter, but it is possible to identify several factors that might cause one utility stock to be considered riskier than another.

On this basis the equation was fitted to data for 69 electric utility companies for each of the years 1958–1962.[26] In every instance the resulting estimate of b was less than 0.5. This finding provides the most cogent evidence that has been adduced for the popular view that the investor is motivated by a strong preference for current income. Nevertheless, despite the greater sophistication of the analysis, it does not wholly escape the problems that bedeviled the earlier exercises. If some of the factors affecting risk were not identified, and if risky concerns tended to distribute a smaller proportion of their earnings, the emphasis that investors place on growth from retention would still be underestimated. Furthermore, if there are any chance errors in the estimates of expected earnings growth, the weighting that the market gives to this growth will again be understated, and so will the required rate of return. Not only would it be very surprising if there were no such estimation errors, but it is noteworthy that the required rates of return that emerged from the analysis were unrealistically low. For these reasons it seems probable that the analysis has considerably exaggerated any market preference for high-payout stocks.

It may not be necessary to adopt such a complex approach in order to avoid the biases inherent in Table 5. The problem posed by temporary fluctuations in earnings can be lessened by measuring both dividends and retentions over a period of several years. Thus one could usefully seek to explain the differences between the prices of a group of stocks by fitting to the data the following equation:

Stock price $= a + b \times$ average dividends per share in 3 prior years $+ c \times$ average retentions per share in 3 prior years.

In this equation, *b* provides an estimate of the rate at which the market capitalizes dividends, and *c* is the multiple applied to retentions.

There is still the problem of allowing for other factors that may affect both the stock price and the dividend decision. One could do so by building each of them into the equation. However, because of the difficulty of knowing what these factors are and how they should be measured, it may be better to incorporate in the equation an item whose value reflects the importance of these other influences. A possible candidate for this position is the average price-earnings multiple during the previous three years. The expanded equation would then read

Stock price $= a + b \times$ average dividends per share $+ c \times$ average retentions per share $+ d \times$ average price-earnings ratio.

This equation was fitted to the stock prices of 255 firms in two different years.[40] In 1961 the market appeared to have capitalized dividends at a multiple of 15.8 and retentions at a multiple of 15.0. In the next year a multiple of 13.9 was indicated for dividends and one of 12.9 for retentions. These results are a far cry from studies that suggested dividends were valued four times as highly as retained earnings, though they still indicate that the market shows some preference for current income.

Probably the most serious objection to this exercise lies in the addition of the price-earnings ratio to the right-hand section of the equation, so that the stock price comes to be represented on both sides of the equation. The danger that this may produce misleading results is heightened in this case by the fact that any relation between stock price and earnings multiple could in part reflect a general preference for dividends or retentions.

A second qualification centers on the procedure of averaging only three years' worth of dividends and retentions. Particularly if management takes future prospects into account in determining the dividend rate, some bias will still be present, for in these circumstances investors would be justified in looking on any increase in the payout ratio as a precursor of rising earnings and would bid up the stock price correspondingly.

If the market does capitalize dividends at a slightly higher rate, then it must be willing to tolerate a lower gross return from high-payout stocks. This could be investigated by fitting to the data an equation of the form

Expected return $\% = a + b \times$ expected payout ratio $+ c \times$ risk.

If b should prove to be negative, there would be additional evidence for the view that the market prefers dividends.

One practical problem in applying this test is that of measuring the return expected from each stock. However, it could be argued that although in any one year the return may be higher or lower than the market anticipates, over the long run it will average out at roughly the expected level. For this reason the expected return for each of nearly 300 stocks between 1946 and 1963 was assumed to be the same as the return actually achieved over these years.[3] The expected payout ratio was also approximated by the average ratio over the period. Finally, instead of building into the equation just one measure of risk, three such measures were used simultaneously. When the equation was fitted to the data, it revealed a slight tendency for the expected rate of return to vary inversely with the proportion of earnings that the company distributed.

Even when, as in this case, a relatively large number of years is used, the averaging procedure is likely to prove a somewhat clumsy method of measuring the company's desired payout ratio. A more efficient technique might be to estimate directly for each firm the earnings that would normally be associated with a given year's dividend. With the aid of this estimate it is possible to fit to the data an equation of the form

Value of firm $= a + b \times$ dividend liberality $+ c \times$ normal earnings $+ d \times$ other influences.

In this instance, b measures the extent to which the payout ratio has an effect on the stock price over and above any information that it provides about the company's normal earning power. An elaboration of this two-stage approach was employed in a study of the dividend policies of 63 electric utility companies in each of the years 1954, 1956, and 1957.[103] Considerable care was taken to avoid the kinds of bias that have beset the other investigations. This time investors appeared to possess a faint preference for companies that distributed only a small proportion of earnings.

Although there may be no single payout rate that investors prefer on the average, it does not follow that they do not care about the dividend policy of the individual firm. In fact, it seems reasonable to suppose that investors would rather see companies in stagnant or declining industries distribute their profits than see them plowed back into unrewarding enterprises. Conversely, where a company is operating in a growth industry with high potential returns on new investment, the market may favor a high rate of retention. Some support for this view was obtained by repeating separately for each of 8 industry groups the exercise described on page 16.[40] Both in 1961 and in 1962 the market appeared to prefer a low rate of distribution from retail, utility, and oil companies but to welcome high payouts from firms in the more mature metal, railroad, and mining industries. The valuation of chemical and transport companies showed no uniform pattern. These findings were reinforced by a set of tests employing data for 5 industry groups in each of the years 1956 and 1958.[55] The market seemed to prefer retentions in the electronic and utility industries and dividends in the relatively stagnant food and steel sectors. The results for the chemical group were again ambiguous. Less satisfactory conclusions emerged when the analysis of rates of return between 1946 and 1963 was extended to individual sectors.[3] This lack of corroboration may not be too significant. Not only were the sample sizes very small, but it is probable that over such a long period the market frequently revised its assessment of which industries possessed the brightest prospects. The weight of evidence therefore suggests that the market welcomes a high rate of investment by companies in expanding industries. This does not, however, imply that investors necessarily prefer such expenditures to be financed from retentions rather than from new issues of stock.

The path that has been traced in this first chapter has been a tortuous and occasionally divided one. Before considering where it has led, it may be worth reviewing the route. The initial discussion indicated that the main reason for an investor to be concerned with the rate of payout lies in the differential rates of tax on dividends and capital gains. This factor is irrelevant to the tax-exempt institution but should be a serious consideration for the wealthy private investor. Estimates of investor tax rates suggested that on the average a dollar of dividends is probably equivalent after tax to about 75 cents of capital gain.

Several scraps of evidence implied that investors are indeed conscious of the tax effect. In particular, the behavior of stocks on ex-dividend dates is consistent with the view that investors treat a dollar of dividends as equal to about 85 cents of capital gain.

This reasoning might lead one to suspect that low-payout stocks would tend to sell at a slight premium. This is in sharp contrast to the traditional argument that investors exhibit a marked preference for dividends. Although a large volume of evidence has been adduced for this popular belief, without exception it is subject to very serious biases. Studies that have sought to avoid these biases have all agreed that there is no

Chapter 2 *The Dividend Decision*

The association between changes in the dividend rate and
changes in the stock price should become somewhat clearer if
one can identify the factors that lead a company to alter its
dividend. Some help on this question was provided by a series
of interviews with the management of 28 companies.[89] The
interviews suggested that the decision was made predominantly in the light of the company's earnings. Stockholders were
regarded as entitled to a fair share of earnings, and their
satisfaction with the conduct of the business was thought to
depend in part on their getting this share. Thus the company's
primary concern was with the proportion of earnings to be distributed rather than with the proportion that ought to be

retained to finance expansion. Two-thirds of the companies indicated that they had a deliberate payout target, and most of the remainder described policies that were consistent with one. Although references to such target ratios are common in company statements, the interviews provided no information as to how the target comes to be set. Usually it appears to have been brought down from Mount Sinai on tablets of stone.

According to this picture, retained earnings were no more than a residual. If they provided insufficient capital for planned expenditure, the firm would seek outside finance or defer the investment rather than revise its dividend policy. This is in accord with studies of capital spending. For example, a series of detailed discussions with 20 firms revealed that projects tend to be classified into two groups.[41] Where the expenditure is routine in character or essential to the firm's competitive position, management is willing to obtain funds from external sources. Only as a last resort will the dividend be cut. In the case of proposals that fall into the discretionary category, more rigorous screening is employed, and the total of such expenditures is kept within the firm's capacity to generate the funds internally.

The dividend survey indicated that the decision as to the appropriate payment was always made in the context of earlier dividends. In other words, corporations considered first whether the level of earnings justified a change in the existing payment and second how large the change should be. The propriety of the newly established rate itself was therefore never called into question. This behavior seems to have arisen from the conviction that most stockholders prefer a reasonably stable income and react adversely to any reduction in dividends. For this reason, most managements tried to avoid changes in the payment that might have to be reversed at a later date. Even if the company's circumstances in one year appeared to warrant a certain change in the dividend, the management chose to make only a partial adjustment in the rate until there was some confirmation that the improved conditions were permanent.

Before one can assess whether this approach to dividends is typical, it is necessary to describe the process in a way that is amenable to testing. According to the survey, corporations adopt a target payout ratio that they apply to current earnings. If dividends were fully adjusted each year to achieve the target level, the payment on any occasion would simply equal the target ratio multiplied by current earnings, and the change in the dividend would consist of the difference between this figure and the previous year's payment. Thus one could write

Dividend change = target ratio × earnings — previous dividend.

However, the interviews also suggested that a conservative bias led companies to adopt only a proportion of this indicated change. If this proportion is termed the "safety factor," the equation becomes

Dividend change = safety factor × (target ratio × earnings — previous dividend).

In addition, there may be some tendency for dividends to drift upward even when earnings are stable, so that

Dividend change = annual drift + safety factor × (target ratio × earnings — previous dividend).

As a first test of the accuracy of this description, the equation was fitted to data for aggregate corporate profits and dividends for the years 1920 to 1941, with the exception of 1936 to 1938, when the undistributed profits tax was levied.[27] Not only was the equation successful in explaining a large part of the movement in dividends during this period, but the values obtained for the annual drift, safety factor, and target payout were all quite plausible. In particular, the estimated target ratio was very close to the long-term average payout ratio.

However, when the exercise was repeated for the 1942–1960 period, the whole theory received a setback. This time an unreasonably high figure for the target ratio was secured, and the equation provided only a mediocre description of dividend behavior. When one looks at the data, it is easy to see why. During this eighteen-year period, corporate earnings increased by only 2% per annum, while dividends rose at an annual rate of almost 6%. It is difficult to argue from these figures that companies were aiming to distribute a constant proportion of earnings.

One possibility is that the liberalization of dividends during the postwar years reflects the fact that the true increase in earnings has been masked by the more generous depreciation provisions. Although the company interviews provided no support for the theory, it could be that managements have regarded the higher depreciation allowances as a cushion that justified higher dividend payments. If companies do take depreciation into account in determining funds available for distribution, the explanatory equation may be modified by substituting cash flow for earnings. The revised equation was fitted to the data for each of the periods 1920–1941 and 1942–1960. The values secured for the three items are shown in Table 6. Thus, in the case of the

TABLE 6. *Estimates of Determinants of Aggregate Dividends*

	Annual Drift (billions of $)	Safety Factor	Target Payout of Cash Flow
1920–1941	−0.03	29%	55%
1942–1960	0.29	54	29

Source: After Brittain.[27] Copyright © 1966 by The Brookings Institution. Adapted by permission.

second period, companies were revealed as aiming to distribute 29% of their cash flow, though their innate caution led them to move only 54% of the way toward this target in any one year. On top of all this, there appeared to be an annual upward drift in payments of $0.29 billion.

These results are more plausible. In particular, it is encouraging that the total sum paid out in dividends was in each period very similar to the estimated target amount. It is equally impressive that in each period the equation was able to explain over 80% of the year-to-year differences in dividend changes. The significance of the figure for annual drift is more doubtful. Not only is the amount very small, but the presence of a dividend term on either side of the equation is liable to impart an upward bias to the estimated drift.[47]

If this description is correct, one might hope to be able to employ the equation developed for the 1942–1960 period to forecast dividend changes in subsequent years. Estimates were therefore derived for aggregate payments in each of the years 1961, 1962, and 1963, on the assumption that cash flow for the current year and dividends for the previous year were known. These estimates were superior to any produced by cruder techniques.

While these findings generally support the view that companies are constantly moving in the direction of distributing a target proportion of cash flow, they do not provide a complete account of the process. For the interwar years the target ratio was estimated at 55%. Over the subsequent period the figure was 29%. It appears, therefore, that the target ratio is not so immutable as was supposed. Since the analysis makes no allowance for possible shifts in this ratio, it cannot offer a very good description of dividend movements during a period in which such a shift occurs. For example, when the equation is fitted to data for the entire 1920–1960 period, the assumption of a constant target rate makes its explanatory power considerably less than when the two subperiods are considered separately.

One possible explanation of these structural shifts in the target payment rests on the fact that dividend income and capital gains are taxed at different rates. If management believes that investors are influenced by this fact, any change in the relative rate of taxation may induce companies to reconsider their dividend policies. Since the early years of the Second World War were marked by a sharp increase in the rate of tax on income, it looks as if this theory may provide the needed explanation of the lower target payout ratio in the following years. When the income tax rate was incorporated in the equation, the fit for the entire period proved to be only marginally inferior to that for the two subperiods.

This finding is consistent with evidence that British dividend payments during the 1950s were in part influenced by the rate of differential profits tax.[49] Nevertheless, the explanation is not altogether convincing. The last chapter uncovered too little evidence of investor attention to tax rates for it to be likely that a change in these rates could have such a major impact on a company's dividend policy. Yet no satisfactory alternative explanation of the fall in the payout ratio has so far been ventured. The yearly level of dividend payments seemed to be affected by some secondary factors. There was, for example, a little evidence that dividend increases were less marked when sales were rising faster than cash flow. This may be a consequence of the need to conserve working capital to finance the increased business, or it may denote a belief that profits based on unusual sales growth are not likely to be maintained. There was also some support for the view that high interest charges may tend to discourage dividend payments by making internal finance more attractive. On the other hand, there was no sign that dividend changes are related to the amount of capital investment or corporate liquidity, so that the data were largely consistent with the picture of retained earnings as simply the residual.

All the evidence has pointed to the fact that the aggregate level of payments depends in part on current earnings and in part on the previous year's dividends. Since the latter in their turn are a function both of that year's earnings and the former level of dividends, the equation that was employed earlier could be expanded to show the change in dividends as equal to a proportion of the change in earnings in the current year plus a smaller proportion of the previous year's change, and so on. Not surprisingly, when the hypothesis has been formulated in this way, it has been no less well supported by the data.[37,74] The statistical tests in themselves cannot satisfactorily determine whether management just looks at the current year's earnings and last year's dividend or whether it employs instead a rough weighted average of past earnings as an estimate of the company's earning power.

The success of this approach in explaining the aggregate level of dividends justifies an investigation of whether it can usefully be extended to the case of the individual firm. If the payment is equal to a weighted average of past earnings, the probability of an increase in the rate should depend to a large extent on whether current earnings have increased, to a somewhat lesser extent on whether the previous year's earnings increased, and so on. When one looks at the dividend policies of nearly 400 major industrial companies during the period 1949 to 1964, it is apparent that they have behaved in this manner.[47] The evidence is summarized in Table 7. It is clear that the likelihood of a dividend increase depends both on the number of occasions on which earnings have risen and on their recency.

This exercise also affords an interesting opportunity to study the way in which dividend policy is affected by the company's

TABLE 7. *Probability of Dividend Change Given Recent Earnings Changes*

Earnings Change			Proportion of Companies		
Current Year	Previous Year	Two Years Earlier	Raising Dividend	Maintaining Dividend	Cutting Dividend
+	+	+	81%	8%	11%
+	+	−	67	15	18
+	−	+	58	17	25
−	+	+	54	15	32
+	−	−	49	18	34
−	+	−	45	19	36
−	−	+	35	17	48
−	−	−	25	25	50

Source: After Fama and Babiak.[47]

size. For this purpose the firms were divided into four groups on the basis of size, and the analysis was repeated separately for each group. Table 8 shows the findings for the largest and smallest firms. Regardless of recent earnings growth, the smaller companies were less ready to change their dividends. Apart from this, their behavior in periods of prosperity was very similar to that of the larger firms. After a succession of poor years, however, the smaller companies proved far more ready to cut their dividends. This behavior is understandable. Such firms can less easily supplement any deficiency in working capital by short-term borrowing and may be less concerned with their stock-market image, so that a dividend reduction may be more necessary and less painful. If stability of income is of paramount importance, an investor would be wise to concentrate on the stocks of large concerns.

Such tests imply that the dividend decision of the individual company can be explained by means of a partial adjustment process, but to learn more about the nature of this process, it is necessary to repeat the analysis that was adopted in the case

TABLE 8. *Probability of Dividend Change by Size of Company Given Recent Earnings Changes*

Earnings Change			Proportion of Companies					
			Raising Div.		Maintaining Div.		Cutting Div.	
Cur-rent Year	Pre-vious Year	Two Years Earlier	Large Cos.	Small Cos.	Large Cos.	Small Cos.	Large Cos.	Small Cos.
+	+	+	84%	78%	5%	12%	11%	10%
+	+	−	68	67	12	16	21	17
+	−	+	67	61	12	17	22	22
−	+	+	57	54	16	16	27	30
+	−	−	57	46	11	22	32	33
−	+	−	52	43	10	21	38	36
−	−	+	46	29	13	22	42	49
−	−	−	39	15	26	33	35	52

Source: After Fama and Babiak.[47]

of aggregate dividends. Since there was little evidence of drift in dividend payments, the problem at issue is whether the actions of any firm can be explained by an equation of the form

Dividend change = safety factor × (target ratio × earnings − previous dividend).

The equation was fitted to the 1947–1964 dividend record of each company. As might be expected, the closeness of the fit differed considerably from one company to another, but on the average the equation was able to explain 43% of the variation in a company's dividend changes. By the same token there were considerable differences in the estimated target ratios and safety factors, but in general firms were shown as aiming to distribute 46% of their earnings and as moving 37% of the way toward this objective in any one year.

In the analysis of aggregate dividends, the equation based on simple net earnings performed relatively poorly in the post-1941 period. The reason was apparently that the liberalization of depreciation allowances had encouraged companies to raise their target payout ratios during this period. In the case of individual firms the use of net earnings figures produced quite good results, and the introduction of depreciation into the equation secured no improvement. In consequence, the effect of depreciation provisions on payout ratios must remain in some doubt.

Both the company interviews and the analysis of aggregate dividends suggested that in determining the appropriate payment, corporations pay no heed to variations in their cash requirements. Correspondingly, the dividend changes of individual companies displayed no significant relation to the variation in capital expenditures.

If this is a correct description of the dividend process for individual firms, the estimates of the target ratio and the safety factor that were derived from the 1947–1964 data should prove helpful in predicting subsequent dividend changes. An estimate of the payment in 1965 was made on this basis for each of the companies. These estimates offered a modest but significant improvement over ones employing cruder techniques.

Management's cautious attitude when altering the dividend rate may stem either from the belief that stockholders prefer gradual changes[148] or from a concern that they may misinterpret abrupt ones.[102] In either case it is unreasonable to suppose that management would determine the appropriate payment solely in the light of recent earnings, without any consideration of the prospects. Indeed, in the last chapter it was suggested that the stock market's reaction to a dividend announcement was colored largely by the belief that the decision conveys some information about the earnings outlook. Unfortunately, very little attempt has been made to determine how far such an attitude is justified. One study of the variations in the aggregate level of dividends during the period 1930 to 1955 concluded that insofar as these variations could not be explained by prior earnings, they were a reflection of management's expectations.[38] Without any adequate alternative measure of these expectations this is difficult to confirm or deny, but the relation between the level of aggregate payments and the subsequent progress of corporate profits was certainly far from obvious.

The evidence concerning individual firms is a little more encouraging. In the first place, it is worth bearing in mind that a firm's dividend rate is often effectively determined by the first quarterly payment. The fact that this rate is quite closely associated with the progress of earnings in that year suggests that the directors are at least taking short-term prospects into account.[74] A study of the distribution policies of 147 British companies offers some support for this view. In 1962 the proportion of earnings distributed varied from 15% to 200%. These differences were probably in some degree attributable to differences in the target payout rate. However, as long as each company moved only gradually toward its target distribution, the payout would also be a reflection of the recent rate of earnings growth. In these circumstances, a sharp rise in earnings would not typically be matched by an equally sharp rise in the dividend, and the payout ratio would decline. In the same way, the payout ratio is liable to be inversely related in some lesser degree to the earnings growth in earlier years. If it is also true that management considers the earnings prospects when setting the dividend rate, differences in the payout ratio might be a portent of future earnings changes. Thus, an unusually low payout could be an indication either that earnings have risen very rapidly or that they are about to decline very rapidly. To test the truth of this assertion, the following equation was fitted to the data:

1962 payout ratio $= a + b \times$ 1961 earnings change $+ c \times$ 1962 earnings change $+ d \times$ 1963 earnings change $+ e \times$ 1964 earnings change.

As expected, the estimates of b and c were both significantly less than 0 and those for d and e were significantly greater than 0. This exercise was repeated for each of the two preceding years with comparable results. All estimates of b and c were positive, and in only one instance was the estimate of d or e other than negative. One final clue was provided by an attempt to explain differences in the rate of growth of 244 American companies during the period 1950–1965.[107] There appeared to be a slight positive association between the payout ratio in any one year and the growth in earnings over the following one, two, or five years. None of this evidence is as strong as one would like it to be, but it does tend to bear out the suggestion that the dividend decision conveys important information about company prospects.

Chapter 3 *Debt and the Stock Price*

Very little is yet known about the general problem of what makes the future of one enterprise less certain than that of another. Consequently, in the absence of any better alternative, many have been led to assume that these risks are revealed in the degree of earnings fluctuation. This may not be a bad approximation, for there is some evidence that the market places more value on the stocks of companies that have relatively consistent records of growth.[20,35,157] Nevertheless, it remains an approximation. The earnings of U.S. Steel or Alcoa may be cyclical and erratic. Yet most investors would agree that these fluctuations are caused largely by temporary shocks that do not reflect on the considerable measure of resilience both companies possess.

On one point at least there is no disagreement. Other things being equal, a company with a high proportion of outstanding debt is more risky than one financed entirely by equity. The effect of such leverage on the stock price is therefore worth considering at some length.

It would seem reasonable to suppose that whenever two companies possess equally good earnings prospects, the market would place more value on the firm that can achieve this expansion without the additional uncertainty imposed by leverage. This can be demonstrated with the aid of the sample of 170 stocks referred to in the introduction to Part I. In each of the years 1961–1965 the degree of leverage exerted a significant downward impact on the multiple, after differences in earnings prospects are taken into account.[35]

The practical importance of this result is limited by the fact that a high rate of earnings growth and a low degree of leverage do not usually go hand in hand. Just as a company cannot distribute a high proportion of its earnings without affecting the future rate of growth, so a company cannot normally issue equity instead of debt without expecting to depress its earnings per share. A more useful question, therefore, is whether the market believes that the risks of leverage are adequately compensated by the prospect of higher earnings. Does the use of leverage tend to raise or lower the price of the stock?

It is possible to envisage a world in which the degree of leverage is at all times wholly irrelevant to the stock price.[106] This would be true of an economy where there is neither taxation nor impediment to the free flow of funds and where all members act in a rational manner. In these circumstances it would make no difference to the more adventurous stockholders whether they themselves borrowed funds or whether the company did so on their behalf. In either case they would be entitled to the company's gross profit less the interest on the outstanding debt. The more cautious stockholders would be equally indifferent to a firm's financial structure. By purchasing both the company's debt and its common stock, they could ensure that they were always entitled to the company's gross profit. Thus, as long as the investor is free to contribute his own leverage or undo that of the company, he should be willing to pay neither more nor less for the stock of a leveraged firm. This would be the case regardless of his aversion to risk.

It is important to bear in mind that although in these circumstances the stock price is not affected by the issuance of debt, earnings per share are likely to be increased thereby. It necessarily follows that the effect of the prospective earnings gain is exactly counterbalanced by a decline in the rate at which these earnings are capitalized.

The precise assumptions that are necessary for this conclusion have been the source of considerable controversy. Certainly they need to be specified more carefully than has been done here. However, this hypothetical case does serve to draw attention to the fact that it is impossible to assess the merits of issuing a particular security solely on the basis of its effect on expected earnings. In particular, it emphasizes that in no circumstances should one assume that debt is a desirable form of financing just because the rate of interest is less than the expected return on capital. For present purposes the model has the additional attraction of providing a framework for considering the effect of leverage in the imperfectly competitive conditions that are encountered in practice. As soon as these imperfections are introduced, it becomes necessary to modify the earlier rigid conclusion.

One unrealistic feature of the model was the stipulation that both companies and individuals are free of taxation.[105,106] Since interest payments are a deductible expense against corporate income tax, it no longer becomes a matter of indifference to the stockholder whether he or the corporation undertakes the borrowing. The benefit of this tax subsidy is likely to be offset in part by the fact that leverage may increase the total amount of personal income tax that is paid, for the whole of the bondholder's income is subject to taxation, whereas the earnings attributable to the stockholder are taxed only if distributed. Nevertheless, as long as the corporate tax rate is greater than the bondholder's personal rate, leverage might be expected to induce a moderate rise in the stock price.

Furthermore, despite their wider legal liability, individuals usually have higher borrowing costs than corporations and may therefore prefer the company to borrow on their behalf. On many occasions borrowing by the investor and by the company may not even be feasible alternatives. If the investor is unable to obtain a personal loan, indirect leverage may be the only method open to him. On other occasions the investor may have the opportunity both to borrow funds and to place the proceeds in the stock of leveraged companies. In either of these circumstances, the leveraged company becomes more attractive to the investor who is willing to accept considerable risks in the hope of very high rates of gain. Such a result would be one more instance of what seems to be a general tendency for these investors to bid up the price of high-risk securities until they offer relatively small improvements in return.

Considerations such as these suggest that whereas it may be relatively simple for an investor to undo the effect of company borrowing by lending an equivalent amount of his own cash, it may not be so easy for him to simulate the effect of such borrowing. If this is so, one might expect the issue of debt to lead to an increase in the price of the stock. The argument is consistent with a popular belief that modest amounts of borrowing enhance the stock price, but it provides no support for the equally common view that beyond a certain point further increments of debt can only have a depressing influence. Since the tax advantage rises in approximately direct proportion to the degree of leverage, increases in corporate borrowing should always, on the face of it, benefit the stockholder. The reason that this may not occur in practice is that most suppliers of fixed-interest capital are reluctant to risk having a defaulting loan on their books. The rigid lending standards that they are led to employ in consequence could cause a shortage of funds available for loan to firms that are already highly leveraged. In any event, the number of companies that allow their borrowing to exceed acceptable conservative standards is still relatively small, so that it is not easy to judge what is the effect of very high degrees of leverage. Such studies as have been made are largely inconclusive.[9]

One way to assess whether modest amounts of debt can affect the total market value of the firm would be to look at a group of companies that were alike in every respect save their capital structure and prospective profits. If the only advantage that the market sees in the use of debt is that it reduces the corporate tax bill, the differences in the total value of each firm's securities should reflect only differences in the after-tax profits that are expected to be available to them. Hence the market value of each firm's securities should constitute the same multiple of the profits available for interest less tax. When plotted in the form of a scatter diagram, the data should lie along a horizontal line, as in Figure 2. If, however, the market believes that leverage has attractions that are over and above the tax advantage, the crosses should form a downward-sloping line.

This approach was employed to investigate the association between leverage and market value of 42 oil companies in 1952–1953.[138] The resulting scatter diagram is reproduced in Figure 3. The horizontal axis marks the ratio of the market value of a firm's senior securities to that of all its securities. The vertical

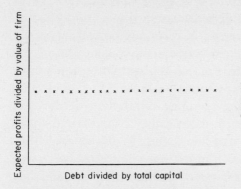

FIGURE 2. Hypothetical market in which value of firm is invariant with use of debt.

axis shows the profits available for interest less tax in the years 1952 and 1953 as a multiple of the company's total market value. Each point on the chart denotes a different company. In contrast to the hypothetical situation illustrated in Figure 2, these points are distributed widely across the graph, but by fitting a line through them it is possible to verify that after allowing for the tax effect there was no tendency for the value of the firm to change with leverage.

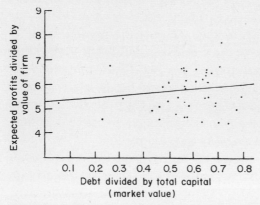

FIGURE 3. The relation between market valuation and financial structure of 42 oil companies in 1953 (after Smith).[138]

A similar test was applied to the value of 43 large electric utilities for the period 1947–1948.[2] Again the average level of profits for the two years was employed as a guide to expected profit. The resulting scatter diagram is shown in Figure 4. In this case also the effect of leverage seems to be confined to the tax advantage.

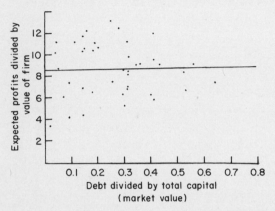

FIGURE 4. The relation between market valuation and financial structure of 43 electric utilities, 1947–1948 (after Allen).[2]

A third test examined the leverage and market valuation of 61 railroad companies in 1956.[9] On this occasion expected profits were approximated by an average of the 1954–1956 levels. The data are plotted in Figure 5. The downward slope of the plotted line suggests a slightly more marked preference for leverage.

These results must be treated with some suspicion. Not only is there a statistical problem in estimating the relation between two ratios comprising the same term, but the application of all three tests fell short of the proposed method in two important respects. In the first place, the market value of the securities was expressed as a ratio of past rather than of expected income. It is probable that expectations are heavily influenced by the recent level of profits, but they are certainly not the same thing. Second, it was stipulated that the companies selected for testing should be alike in all respects except for their capital structure. Although each group of companies was fairly homogeneous in character, the wide scatter of the points in all these diagrams is testimony to the fact that the variations in market price were in part the result of other unwanted differences in their operations.

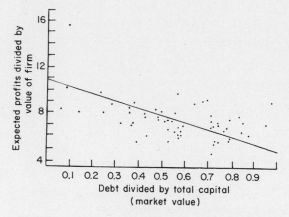

FIGURE 5. The relation between market valuation and financial structure of 61 railroads in 1956 (after Barges).[9] Copyright © 1963 by Prentice-Hall, Inc. Adapted by permission.

It is obviously impossible in practice to find a group of companies that are identical in all respects, and it may not matter much to the conclusions. However, there are circumstances in which these approximations could result in errors. For example, the expected profits of companies whose products are subject to wide fluctuations in demand are likely to be less highly valued by the market than those of their more stable counterparts. If these companies are also distinguished by a high proportion of loan capital, then it might obscure any tendency for the market to exhibit a special preference for leveraged companies. This bias is illustrated by Figure 6. If either group of companies is considered separately, a clear association between leverage and market valuation is revealed. Yet, when the two groups are combined, this association disappears. The horizontal line passed through both sets of points appears to indicate that apart from the tax effect, leverage has no consistent impact on the stock price.

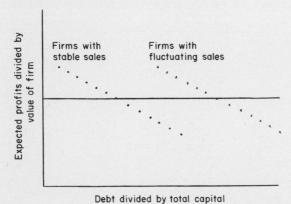

FIGURE 6. Hypothetical illustration of the effect of unwanted heterogeneity (after Barges).[9] Copyright © 1963 by Prentice-Hall, Inc. Adapted by permission.

Whether the three tests were in fact distorted in this way depends on whether companies with fluctuating sales tend also to issue large amounts of debt. To some extent the opposite seems to be true, for highly cyclical companies have been found to shun the additional risks imposed by leverage.[23,57] However, in each of the preceding examples leverage was measured by the ratio of the market value of senior securities to the market value of all securities, which would automatically have caused a company to appear more highly leveraged if the stock stood at a low price.

This bias would not result only from differences in operating risks. Any characteristic that would have caused the profits of some companies to be less highly valued than others would also have caused these companies to appear more highly leveraged. It is therefore quite possible that if allowance could be made for this effect, each of the tests would show a greater preference for leverage.

In the case of the 61 railroad companies an attempt was made to avoid this problem by recalculating leverage in terms of book values.[9] Figure 7 demonstrates that when measured in

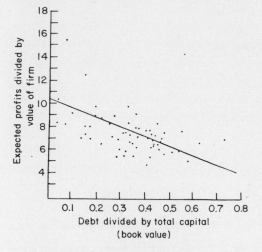

FIGURE 7. A further test of the relation between valuation and financial structure of 61 railroads in 1956 (after Barges).[9] Copyright © 1963 by Prentice-Hall, Inc. Adapted by permission.

this way, debt appears to have more impact on market valuation. This test is more convincing, but it certainly does not escape the problem of heterogeneity. In particular, it is possible that a bias in the other direction has been caused by the tendency for leverage to be preferred by companies that are subject to fewer operating risks.

Instead of looking at the effect of leverage on the total value of the firm, one could equally well look at its effect on the price-earnings ratio. Corporate borrowing usually raises the level of expected earnings, as a result of the leverage effect and the tax subsidy. Therefore, unless there is an equivalent fall in the rate at which these earnings are capitalized, the price of the stock must rise. An analysis of the relation between the price-earnings ratio and the book debt–equity ratio in the department store industry and the cement industry in 1956 concluded that in neither case was there any significant propensity for the multiple to fall as the amount of debt is increased.[9] This suggests that the market preference for leverage goes beyond the tax advantage.

These two tests, like the previous ones, sought to circumvent the problem of extraneous influences on the stock price by choosing, as far as possible, companies that differed only in their leverage and expected profits. It has to be assumed that if the companies do vary in other respects, these differences occur equally in leveraged and unleveraged firms. An alternative, and more satisfactory, approach is to admit the impossibility of finding a completely homogeneous group of firms and to concentrate instead on determining how the more important factors affect the multiple. For example, one might investigate the suggestion that the price-earnings ratio is affected by such considerations as the past price trend, the payout ratio, the earnings stability, the company size, and the degree of leverage. For this purpose data were collected for 56 industrial stocks for each of the years 1954–1957.[14] The following equation was then fitted:

Price/recent earnings $= a + b \times$ past price trend $+ c \times$ payout ratio $+ d \times$ earnings stability $+ e \times$ company size $+ f \times$ book value of debt/market value of equity.

When allowance was made for these additional influences, there was no noticeable tendency for the price-earnings multiple to decline with leverage. Yet at least one major difficulty remains. Since debt was considered independently of earnings stability, the analysis has indicated only that apart from any effects associated with diminished earnings stability, the market price can be expected to reflect fully the increase in earnings arising from the use of debt. Because investors were also shown to prefer stable earnings, it seems probable that the use of debt raises the stock price less than it raises earnings.

A similar approach to the problem started from the assumption that the price-earnings ratio is a function of the earnings record, the payout ratio, the firm's size, and the degree of leverage.[159] In addition, allowance was made for the possibility that other unknown factors might affect the stocks of companies in particular industries. An equation linking the price-earnings ratio to these possible influences was fitted to the data for 50 companies for each of the years 1956, 1958, 1961, and 1963. In each period leverage was revealed as exerting a downward impact on the multiple after the effect of all the other factors was taken into account. Since the other factors on this occasion included the additional growth in earnings resulting from the use of debt, this outcome is fully to be expected; the most notable feature of the experiment was that the reduction in the multiple was more than outweighed by the beneficial effect that debt had on earnings. On balance it appeared that the stock price increased less than earnings but more than the tax advantage alone would justify.

One interesting aspect of this study was the decision to measure leverage in terms of the proportion of profit that would have been absorbed by interest payments in years when earnings fell significantly below trend. Since this definition takes into account the fact that debt entails fewer risks for companies whose profits are not subject to major gyrations, it may provide a useful guide to the quality of a corporate bond. However, for present purposes a measure that lumps together operating and financial risk has definite disadvantages.

A recurring problem in every effort to measure the importance of a company's financial structure is that although the value placed on the firm depends to a large extent on the long-run earnings expectation, no record of the latter is available. Yet the use of past levels of earnings may lead to biased results. One way to escape from this impasse may be to estimate the prospective level of long-run sustainable earnings from the information contained in such features as the level of dividends or the rate of asset growth. Given such a measure of expected earnings, it should be possible to isolate the effect of leverage on the value of the firm by fitting some such equation as this to the data:

Value of firm $= a + b \times$ (expected net profits $+$ interest) $+ c \times$ preferred stock $+ d \times$ asset growth $+ e \times$ size $+ f \times$ outstanding debt.

A rather complex study along these lines was made of 63 electric utility companies in each of the years 1954, 1956, and 1957.[103] The results were consistent with the view that leverage enhances the value of the firm only to the extent of the tax advantage.

Not all the studies described in this chapter have come to the same conclusion. Yet it is important not to let these differences obscure the fact that on one point there is general agreement. Reasonable amounts of corporate borrowing have been shown to increase the value of the common stock at least to the extent of the reduction in corporate tax payments. In consequence, firms that as a matter of policy do not exploit the government subsidy on borrowing are acting against the best interests of their shareholders.

Divergences of view appear when one proceeds to inquire whether the market places a higher value on leveraged companies than the tax advantage alone would justify. If this added premium does exist, it is certainly not very large, so that there is no reason to believe that leveraged stocks are any more highly valued than other high-risk securities.

If it is accepted that leverage affects the stock price mainly through the tax advantage, then one can establish some general criteria for deciding on an appropriate capital structure. In these circumstances the value of the firm remains largely independent of the way in which it is financed, except insofar as the financing scheme can actually increase the company's gross profits less tax. Financing plans should therefore be guided by this principle rather than by the misguided belief that the value of a company, like that of a deodorant, depends mainly on the package.

Chapter 4 *Mergers and Acquisitions*

Merger activity appears to be subject to periodic fluctuations that correspond roughly to the business cycle.[108] However, in the postwar years the number of mergers rose sharply, until in 1968 they absorbed an unprecedented 2400 industrial companies. The role and impact of this development are beyond the scope of this book. Nevertheless, some of the reasons adduced for mergers raise the same kinds of issues as the other chapters in this section, so that it is worth considering briefly whether a merger of itself can raise the value of a company's stock.

Many of the arguments for growth through acquisition lay stress on the fact that the combined company may be able to

48

secure a higher return on capital than if the firms continued to operate separately. For example, the merger may lead to a reduction in competition and so allow the company to increase the price of its products. This motive acted as a major stimulus to merger activity in the early years of the century, though subsequent antitrust legislation has severely limited the opportunities for such behavior. A merger may also be justified if it assists a company to reach a more efficient size, and for this reason recent mergers in the British computer, automobile, textile, and electrical industries have received government encouragement. However, too little is known of the relation between size and profitability in particular industries to permit any generalizations on the scope for such gains, although it is worth bearing in mind that the merger as such does not bring economies of scale. These follow only when the product line is rationalized or the sales forces integrated or production redistributed. Such tasks are not easily accomplished. Mergers may also contribute to a higher return on investment if they lead to fuller utilization of existing capacity. A typical example is the case of the firm with the underemployed sales force. Acquisition of a company with a related product line may be an effective means of overcoming the problem.

These arguments apply to only a small proportion of the mergers that have been consummated in recent years. Partly because of governmental impediments to horizontal or vertical integration, the postwar period has been characterized by a rapid growth in conglomerate mergers. On a conservative interpretation of the term, over 40% of recent mergers have taken this form. Because the process extends the company's product line into unrelated areas, it cannot easily be justified on the grounds that it reduces competition or allows economies of scale. In only a very special sense can the conglomerate hope to eliminate spare capacity, for typically the head office itself is the only resource that is shared by the operating divisions. Yet, rather than permit a reduction in the number of administrative staff, the process of diversification is likely to increase the complexity of their task. Nevertheless, the principal case for the conglomerate merger is that it may enable more effective use to be made of an exceptionally able management. This is most likely to occur when the acquisition offers the only practical method of ridding the acquired company of a president who persistently acts against the best interests of his shareholders. There is some disagreement about the opportunities for management improvement offered by these means. The belief that managerial skills are readily transferable may be a myth, for the ability to make correct decisions is intimately bound up with the manager's detailed knowledge of the peculiarities of his own business. If he is called upon to make decisions in unrelated areas, his judgment will almost inevitably suffer.

Even if the conglomerate merger does not lead to increased efficiency, the stockholders of the acquiring company may still benefit if the purchase can be made at a favorable enough price. However, the business of looking for undervalued stocks is a competitive one, and the corporate bidder has few natural advantages. Not only may he find it difficult to obtain impartial sources of information about companies, but when he shows his hand, he is liable to cause the market to reevaluate the stock or to induce a competitor to enter a further bid. Moreover, once a company has been acquired, it cannot be disposed of easily. Perhaps the single advantage that the corporate bidder possesses is the fact that he can pay for his investments with currency whose value he is best equipped to judge.

A policy of diversification by merger is sometimes justified on the grounds that the corporation's existing business offers too little opportunity for the profitable employment of the company's funds. It is at this point that one encounters a divergence of interest between the management and the shareholders. If the continued growth of the corporation is admitted as an end in itself, a plausible case may be made for a policy of acquisition. However, the price of common stock is likely to be better protected by an increase in the payout ratio or by the repurchase of stock.

A similar but more popular argument stresses the fact that diversification insures the company against the effect of a setback in any one sector. This again is a perfectly valid argument if the perpetuation of the firm is regarded as an end in itself. Otherwise, in a rational market it should make little difference whether the diversification is performed by the company or left to the investor. Indeed, in certain circumstances the flexibility of homemade diversification may be an advantage.

In weighing these suggested benefits it is important to remember that the acquirer can usually expect to pay a premium over the existing market price. Several studies of mergers during the postwar period have indicated that the average premium has been in the region of 25% and that in approximately one-fifth of the instances it has been in excess of 50%.[16,61,92,94,156] This constitutes prima facie evidence that the stockholders of the acquired companies have for the most part benefited from the mergers. The much more interesting question is whether the acquiring company likewise profits from its actions. Since the potential gains are likely to be greatest where the merger does not involve product extension, it may be useful to inquire first into the effects of such mergers.

Commercial banks have not been left behind in the postwar merger wave.[32] Between 1950 and 1962 nearly 2000 banks with resources of over $40 billion were absorbed by other banks. In most cases the acquiring companies appear to have paid a sizable premium for their rivals. In return, they presumably expected to realize economies of scale while at the same time removing a competitor. To assess the effects of this activity, an analysis was made of the record of 165 large commercial banks during this period. Approximately a third of these banks made no acquisitions. Their earnings per share rose over the decade by 99%. Another third acquired one or two rival banks. Their earnings rose by 66%. The remainder entered into three or more mergers and achieved an earnings growth of 63%. These quite significant differences suggest that the economies effected by merging were rather less than the companies anticipated. Consequently, it is not surprising that the greatest appreciation was shown by the stocks of banks that relied solely on internal growth. These issues appreciated 101% over the period, the stocks of banks participating in one or two mergers gained 71%, and those of the remainder rose 59%. Broadly similar findings were secured when the banks were analyzed separately according to their geographical location or the state banking regulations.

There is some reason to suspect that this sample may have consisted principally of the most successful of the nonmerging banks. Yet this is not the only evidence to cast doubt on the merits of growth through merger with competitive companies. Between 1955 and 1961 there were 7 occasions on which two advertising agencies joined forces to produce a firm with total billings in excess of $10 million.[71] The solid line in Figure 8 shows the average growth in the revenues of these firms from four years before the merger until four years after. For comparison, the dotted line depicts the fortunes of pairs of comparable agencies that remained independent, and the broken line represents the progress of single agencies that were as large as the combined firms. In the years before they were united, the merging agencies grew at a rate similar to that of their larger competitors but more slowly than that of their nearest equivalents. In the following years the merging firms fared significantly less well than either of the other two groups. In all but 1 of the 7 instances the merger heralded a period of clearly inferior performance in terms of revenues. It is pos-

sible that in terms of profits the picture would have been somewhat different, but the gross profit and cost structures of advertising firms are so closely determined that it would have
been very difficult for the combining agencies to increase their
margins sufficiently to make up for the shortfall in billings.

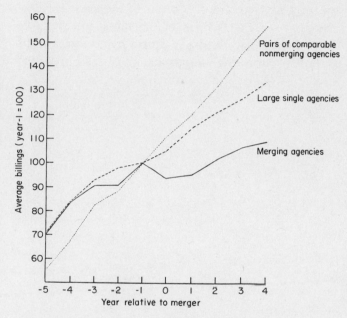

FIGURE 8. The effect of mergers in the advertising industry, 1955–
1961 (after Johnson and Simon).[71]

It has to be admitted that the banking and advertising industries are unusual in many respects and that in both cases there
appear to be special objections to a policy of growth through
merger. Yet the important fact is that these disadvantages do
not seem to have prevented the mergers' occurring with some
frequency. This does not bode well for any analysis that also
comprehends conglomerate mergers.

It might be well to begin such an investigation by considering the short-run effects on the stock price. This can be done by looking at 35 mergers between New York Stock Exchange companies during the period 1961–1965.[16] For purposes of comparison a second group of companies was selected. They did not engage in merger activities but were as far as possible similar to the merging companies in terms of industry, quality, size, and sales growth. The performance of the acquired issues relative to that of their equivalents is shown by the dotted line in Figure 9. Shortly before the announcement of the impending

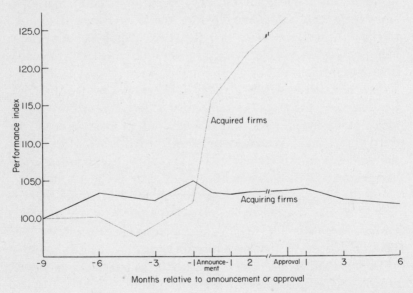

FIGURE 9. Relative performance of stocks of acquiring and acquired firms (after Block).[16]

merger the stock price began to rise. The significant improvement in price in the month before the public disclosure seems to point either to buying by the acquiring firm or to some leakage of information. The principal rise, however, occurred in the month of the announcement, when the stocks on the average appreciated 13%. Since the merger negotiations were in every case successful, it is not surprising to see that the stocks continued to appreciate as the progress of the negotiations became known. However, an investor could have profited from these later gains only if he had managed to avoid other situations where the merger talks were eventually broken off.

The solid line in Figure 9 depicts the performance of the stocks of the acquiring companies relative to that of their near equivalents. These issues behaved in a much less dramatic fashion, and at no point did they depart by more than 2% from their level six months before the announcement of the merger. It therefore seems that the stockholders of the acquiring company do not customarily greet the news with any degree of enthusiasm.

This reaction is equally obvious in the case of tender offers.[110] For example, during 1968 and early 1969 there occurred 20 major cash tender offers, which sought on an average nearly a third of the target company's outstanding shares. For this stock the bidder paid a price that was 18% above the market level on the previous day. The market apparently was not convinced of the wisdom of this premium, for by the end of the month only 2 of the stocks stood above the tender price, and the average level was 10% below. Six months after the offer the stocks remained 10% below the tender price.

To see whether such market hesitancy is justified, one needs to look at the long-term impact of acquisitions. For this purpose an analysis was made of the merger activity of 478 large industrial firms during the period 1951–1961.[119] The firms were segregated into four groups according to the number of companies that they acquired during this period. The average ten-year change in the stock price of each group is shown in Table 9. The results are not easy to interpret. On the one hand, the stockholder seems to have fared much better where

TABLE 9. *Average Annual Appreciation of 478 Stocks, 1951–1961, Grouped According to Merger Activity*

	No Mergers	1–5 Mergers	6–10 Mergers	11+ Mergers
No. of stocks	48	214	142	74
Appreciation (%)	+22.8	+12.7	+13.2	+15.1

Source: After Reid.[119]

the growth was purely internal; on the other, it looks as if a very active merger policy is preferable to a more modest approach. The difference in the performance of the merging and nonmerging companies is somewhat too pronounced to be credible and suggests the possibility of some bias in the sample; it was based on the *Fortune* list of large companies in 1961. Since a firm that did not engage in acquisitions is likely to have become large only if it also increased its equity earnings, the sample may well include only the most successful among these firms. This suspicion is partly confirmed by the fact that the whole group appreciated much more rapidly than Standard & Poor's Index. Indeed, by this yardstick all four categories of stock performed well.

Even if this bias does exist, it should not create such serious problems if one were simply to inquire which form of merger proved to be the most successful. Table 10, therefore, shows

TABLE 10. *Average Annual Appreciation of 430 Stocks, 1951–1961, Grouped According to Type of Merger Activity*

	Horizontal	Vertical	Product-Related	Conglomerate
No. of stocks	195	22	167	46
Appreciation (%)	+12.6	+9.3	+12.9	+18.2

Source: After Reid.[119]

the average change in the stock price according to the character of the firm's acquisition policy. The surprising thing about the result is that it is the conglomerate merger that seems to convey the greatest stockholder benefits. However, at this point another difficulty looms up. The analysis provides no indication of the extent to which these price movements occurred before the merger. This omission may mean that the conclusions drawn from Table 9 are slightly distorted, but the chances of misconstruction are far larger in the present case, for it seems only too likely that conglomerate acquisitions are made after a relative improvement in the stock price.

Selection bias is not a serious worry in the case of two similar studies of the effect of mergers. One of these examined the performance of the common stocks of 43 acquiring companies over a period that began two years before the merger and ended at least two years after.[68] In each case the rate of return was compared with the average return of all New York Stock Exchange (NYSE) issues belonging to the same industry group. In only 10 cases did the stock of the acquiring firm show the superior investment performance, and on the average its rate of return was 10% below that of the industry group.

The other analysis considered 21 large industrial corporations that expanded significantly by means of acquisition during the years 1946 to 1960.[79] For each company the average level of earnings in the five postmerger years was expressed as a proportion of the average level in the preceding five years. These growth rates were then compared with the equivalent figures for nonmerging but otherwise similar firms. The results are shown in the first column of Table 11. In 12 of the 21 cases the earnings growth of the merging company was inferior to that of the company that relied primarily on internal expansion. On the average, the former group showed a relative decline in earnings of 1%. The second column in the table shows

TABLE II. *Growth in Earnings and Stock Price of Merging Company Relative to That of Nonmerging Company*

Merging Company	Nonmerging Company	Relative Earnings Change (%)	Relative Price Change (%)
PhilMorr	Am Tob	+1	−9
Nat Distil	DistSeag	−36	−40
McCrory	GrantW	−4	−17
Revlon	AvonPd	+17	−77
Sunray Oil	Richfd Oil	−21	−8
Pure Oil	Sun Oil	−14	+3
Beech-Nut	Wrigley	−5	+25
HookerC	Wyand Ind	−18	NA
Merck	ParkeDav	+10	+35
Allis Chalm	CaterTr	−63	−57
NatGyps	USGypsm	−13	0
J Morrell	Hormel GA	+43	+91
SunshBis	Un Bis	+29	+29
FedMog	Timken	−8	−8
Ideal Cem	LehPCem	−8	−5
Det Steel	McLouth	−58	−46
Acme St	GraniteC	−25	−59
Am Ag Chem	Va Chemcl	+28	+13
Assd DG	MarshFd	+8	+35
Nat Tea	Gt A & P	+41	+53
StokeVC	Libb McN	+80	+5

Source: After Kelly.[79]

the five-year change in the stock price of the merging companies as a percentage of the change in the stock price of their competitors. The results are similar. In just over half of the cases the stock of the merging firm showed a relative decline, with an average falloff of 2%. Thus, whether measured in terms of earnings or stock price, the acquisition policy seems to have induced an insignificant fall in the relative rate of growth. It is interesting to note that the mergers undertaken by the top three or four companies in the table were largely conglomerate in character. The performance of these firms was markedly inferior to that of the other companies, although the difference is not statistically significant.

The validity of this kind of exercise depends on the extent to which the companies chosen for comparison resemble the merging firms in every respect except their attitude toward acquisitions. This difficulty might be avoided if one were to compare the returns obtained by shareholders in the postmerger years with those obtained before the announcement of the merger. This approach too has its problems, for it is possible that firms contemplate merger only following an unusual rise or fall in the price of their stock. Nevertheless, it may help to provide some check on earlier findings. With this in view, an analysis was made of a sample of 34 companies listed on the NYSE that entered into mergers during the 1950s.[132] In half the cases the shareholder received a higher return over the five-year period ending six months before the announcement of the merger than he did over the succeeding five years. As in the previous investigation, the mergers between companies with related product lines appeared to be marginally more successful. Quite apart from the possible bias already mentioned, this test is once again too limited in scope to provide any definitive answers, but it does furnish a little more reinforcement for earlier results.

More comprehensive evidence regarding the question is contained in a study of 82 mergers occurring between 1954 and 1967.[92] Unfortunately for the present purpose, this analysis was concerned only with the experience of shareholders who exchanged their stock in the acquired company for relatively complicated assets such as convertible preferred stock, convertible debentures, or warrants. Over the two years following the consummation of the merger these securities appreciated by an average of 9.5% per annum. Over the same period Standard & Poor's Composite Index appreciated by an average of

7.4%. The contrast between the two groups of securities would probably be even more marked if allowance were made for the difference in dividend and interest payments. Since in most of these cases the shareholders in the acquired firm were rewarded with convertible bonds and preferred stocks, it is likely that the common stock of the acquiring company also fared a little better than the index. Whether or not this was a consequence of the merger is more questionable. If the choice of relatively complicated forms of financing is an indication that the firms are highly leveraged and willing to take above-average risks, then the high rates of return are only to be expected. In view of this problem one can probably conclude little more than that the mergers had no great effect one way or the other on the stockholder's return.

The discussion at the beginning of this chapter implied that a company usually justifies an acquisition policy in one of three ways. Either it hopes to reduce its risks by diversification, or it believes that the acquired stock is undervalued relative to its own, or it expects the merger to lead to improved efficiency. Since the investor can equally well undertake his own diversification, he would be foolish to pay to have the company do it for him. On the other hand, if the management is right in its analysis, acquisitions made for the other two reasons should lead to a rise in the price of the stock.

The high premiums paid to the shareholders of the acquired company create a strong presumption that they fare very well from the merger. The performance of the acquiring firm proved far less easy to assess. Certainly there was no indication of any unusual rise in its earnings or stock price, and there was some suggestion that the merger tends to precede a slightly inferior rate of growth. It would be foolish to conclude from this that the shareholder cannot expect to benefit in individual cases, for many mergers are clearly well conceived. One of two things must therefore follow. Either an equally large number of mergers are ill advised, or companies tend to expand through merger when the prospects for their existing business are deteriorating.

The evidence was not sufficiently comprehensive to permit any useful judgment on whether certain forms of combination are more efficient than others, though it was apparent that any advantages that the shareholder derived from the merger were directly linked to the resultant growth in earnings. There was no indication that the market places more value on the earnings of companies that achieved diversification by merger. Therefore, mergers that are inspired only by the desire to diversify or employ surplus cash or project a more aggressive image seem unlikely to bring a rise in the price of the stock.

The fact that growth through acquisition is no more effective than that from internal resources is perhaps not surprising. There is no reason to suppose that secondhand assets are a better value than new ones. The suggestion that mergers may portend a below-average rate of growth is more disturbing, but without knowing how rapidly the companies would have grown in the absence of the acquisition, one should be cautious about assuming that their actions are against the stockholder's interests. There is even less reason to suppose that mergers are detrimental to the investing public as a whole, for any losses to the acquiring firms seem to be fully counterbalanced by the gains to the shareholders of the acquired companies. The fact that the investor does not necessarily possess management's concern with corporate power and growth always creates a potential conflict, but there is no evidence to suggest that this has serious economic consequences.

Chapter 5 *Splits and Stock Dividends*

Splits and stock dividends change neither the real assets of the corporation nor the division of ownership. For a large concern the expenses involved can amount to several hundred thousand dollars. Yet there is a not uncommon belief that they confer important substantive benefits on the stockholder which are reflected in the price of the security. Attempts to define these benefits have not been altogether convincing. Some have pointed to the enhanced marketability that accompanies the lower stock price, while others have simply confined themselves to the rather unenlightening assertion that stockholders "like splits because in buoyant markets split shares normally increase in value." [13]

The case for stock dividends has been supported by analogy to cash dividends, a confusion that companies have often helped to perpetuate.[152] For example, in 1959 the chairman of Rohr Aircraft rallied his stockholders with the assurance that the stock dividend would offer them "a greater return while at the same time conserving cash to finance the company's anticipated growth," and in the same year the president of Mohasco observed that the stock dividend would "provide shareholders with tangible evidence of the proposed investment by issuing additional shares to them and by placing this investment on a dividend paying basis."

If these claims are correct, it is possible that when a stock is split or goes ex a stock dividend, the price declines by less than the theoretical amount. This question may be answered by an analysis of all stock dividends of 5% or more issued by NYSE companies during the years 1951–1954.[10] The actual reduction in price was measured by comparing the opening price on the ex-dividend date with the closing price on the previous day. The theoretical reduction was defined as the amount of the stock dividend less the full amount of any cash dividend that may have been going ex at the same time. For each of the 224 stocks, the actual fall in price was expressed as a percentage of this theoretical decline; the percentages were then averaged to produce the results shown in Table 12. In the case of the larger stock dividends, the price fell by the entire amount of the dividend. The decline appeared to be somewhat less for the 5% stock dividends. However, half of these were accompanied by cash payments, and if a rough adjustment is made for the fact that the price usually falls by less than the gross value of any cash distribution, it is clear that the decline induced by the stock dividend was very close indeed to the theoretical 5%.

It is unrealistic to suppose that the effects of each distribution are necessarily confined to the ex-dividend date. It may

TABLE 12. *Price Decline of Stock Dividend Stocks on Ex-Dividend Date*

Size of Stock Dividend	Number of Instances	Average Price Decline as Percentage of Theoretical Decline
5%	104	94.8%
10%	62	100.8
All others	58	100.0
Total	224	97.4%

Source: After Barker.[10]

therefore be instructive to look at the behavior of 940 stocks during the months leading up to and following a stock dividend or split.[48] In each instance at least five shares were distributed for every four previously outstanding, and the sample covered substantially all the distributions of this size occurring on the New York Stock Exchange between 1927 and 1959.

One objection simply to looking at the behavior of each stock over the period of the split is that any effect on the price is liable to be obscured by fluctuations in the level of the market. A rough-and-ready way to adjust for these might be to express each price as a proportion of the market index. Although this method will be employed frequently in the following chapters, it does assume that the market has the same effect on each stock. This is not the case. Some stocks are much more aggressive than others and respond more sharply to market fluctuations. If it were possible to measure the way in which each stock normally reacted to any market change, one could assess more accurately how far any variation in price over the period of the split was the result of market movements. Figure 10 illus-

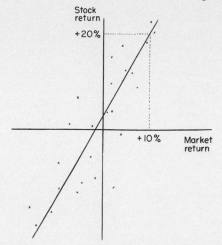

FIGURE 10. Hypothetical example of relation between returns from stock and returns from market.

trates a useful approach to the problem. The vertical axis depicts the monthly return from a hypothetical stock, and the horizontal axis shows on the same scale the corresponding returns from a hypothetical market index. Each point represents the outcome for a different month during the 1927–1960 period, excluding the months close to the split. By passing a line through these points an estimate may be obtained of the typical effect on the price of the stock of any move in the overall market. For example, in the present instance a 10% rise in the market tended to be associated with a 20% appreciation in the price of the stock. Since these relationships do not change greatly over time, it is reasonable to assume that in the months surrounding the split, a 10% gain in the market would continue to lead to a 20% rise in the stock price. If the split has any impact on the value of the stock, it should be observable in the extent to which the price change differs from this expected value.

In this way it was possible to estimate for each of the 940 stocks the price movement that would have occurred during

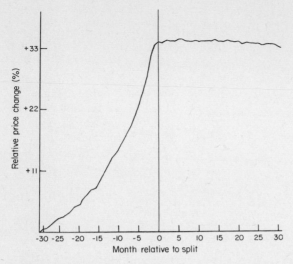

FIGURE 11. Relative performance of 940 stocks over the period of a split (after Fama, Fisher, Jensen, and Roll).[48]

the period of the split if the stock had simply responded in its normal fashion to market fluctuations. Figure 11 shows the average amount by which prices differed from this expected level. In other words, it depicts the relative performance of a portfolio of stocks each of which was acquired 30 months before the occurrence of a split. For much of this time investors could not have been aware of the impending issue, so that the split could not have been responsible for the unusual appreciation that characterized the initial months. It seems, therefore, that directly or indirectly stock splits must be a consequence of rising stock prices. This is borne out by Figure 12, which demonstrates that throughout the years 1927–1959 there was also an association between the level of the market and the number of splits that occurred. In sum, therefore, stock splits seem to have taken place predominantly during buoyant mar-

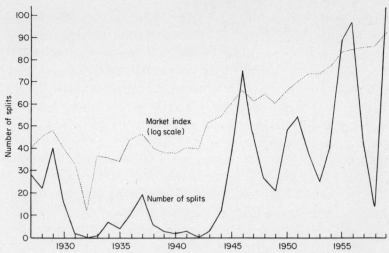

FIGURE 12. Relation between number of splits on the New York Stock Exchange and the level of the market (after Fama, Fisher, Jensen, and Roll).[48]

kets, and the particular stocks involved have been ones that have performed unusually well in these periods.

Returning to Figure 11, one can see that this abnormal appreciation accelerated in the months immediately preceding the split. However, at this point the improvement ceased. Though individual securites may have continued to rise relative to the market, no general price trend is apparent. Indeed, at no time during the next two and a half years did the prices vary on the average by even as much as 1% from the level at the time of the split.

At first sight this result is unexpected, for the firms continued to experience unusual prosperity. For example, 672 out of the 940 companies increased their dividends by an above-average amount in the year following the split. On most occasions this would produce a significant rise in price, but in the case of the split stocks it looks as if the dividend increase caused no surprise. This can only be because the announcement of the split was accompanied by an explicit promise of higher dividends and earnings, or because it was interpreted by the market as foreshadowing such good news. If this is so, the appreciation that immediately precedes the split may have nothing to do with the split as such but may stem merely from the fact that the company's action is regarded as a gesture of confidence in the future.

Figure 13 isolates the price movement of the stocks that did provide an above-average increase in dividends. It is noticeable that during the last few months before the split they

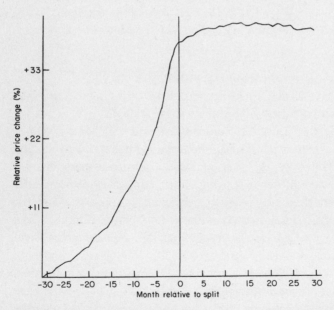

FIGURE 13. Relative performance of 672 stocks for which a split was succeeded by a relative increase in the dividend (after Fama, Fisher, Jensen, and Roll).[48]

appreciated more rapidly than the entire group. Several things may have caused investors to be more confident about these stocks; for example, some additional encouragement may have been given by a company statement at the time of the split. In any case, the significant point about this behavior is that it supports the view that the price movement at the time of the split is a consequence only of the extent to which investors are led to revise their assessment of the stock's outlook.

Figure 14 also accords well with this theory. It portrays the price movement of the much smaller number of stocks where no relative increase in dividends was forthcoming. The fact that these issues rose at all in the presplit months is a sign that at the time the investor could not always identify them. However, over the following year, as the market realized its hopes were misplaced, these stocks fell back in price until they stood at the same level as five months before the split.

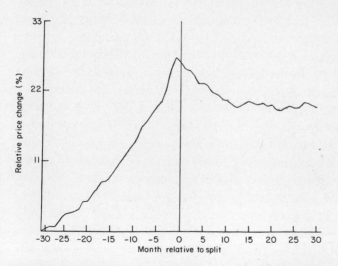

FIGURE 14. Relative performance of 268 stocks for which a split was not succeeded by a relative increase in the dividend (after Fama, Fisher, Jensen, and Roll).[48]

The absence of any general tendency for a split to be followed by a price rise or fall suggests that it is not possible to profit from knowledge of a split after it has taken place. Yet the few months before its occurrence were marked by a sharp appreciation in price. Since the market typically became aware of future stock splits about two months before the issue date, this observation might appear to justify a policy of purchasing stocks after the announcement of a split and holding them until it occurred. Unfortunately, this does not follow. It is true that on the average the stocks appreciated during the two months before the split, but this does not mean that each stock did so. There is a likelihood that the only issues to rise in price during this period were those that delayed announcing their intention until just before the split date.

To determine whether it is possible to achieve superior profits by buying the stocks immediately after the announcement to split, it was necessary to repeat the exercise using the publication month as the bench mark instead of the split month. This was done only for 52 of the 940 stocks. On the average, these issues appreciated steadily up to the time of the announcement but showed no consistent trend thereafter. Some more evidence on this question is provided by an analysis of 100 stocks that split at least two for one between 1946 and 1957.[13] In this case a rough adjustment was made for the effect of market movements by dividing the change in the price of each stock by the change in the appropriate Standard & Poor's industry index. From eight weeks before the announcement date to the day following the announcement, 86% of the stocks registered relative gains. In contrast, over the succeeding eight weeks only 43% of the stocks outperformed the index. Neither this exercise nor the preceding one made any allowance for the fact that the company may sometimes reveal its intention to split before the formal announcement date. Nevertheless, it seems fairly clear that knowledge of an impending split can be put to profitable use only if it has not been widely disseminated.

The evidence presented here has given strong support to the idea that splits confer no significant additional benefits on the stockholder. Once again, therefore, the conclusion seems to be that market values depend on real considerations and cannot be permanently altered by variations in the packaging. The bulk of the associated stock price movement is prompted by the market's realization that splits are generally an indication of company prosperity. Consequently, managements should avoid splitting their stock in the face of deteriorating prospects. It is, however, very debatable whether even in more favorable circumstances the stock split has any advantage over cheaper and more overt expressions of confidence.

This chapter has raised some issues that will recur frequently in those following. The fact that on the average no abnormal price movement occurred after a split is testimony to the efficiency with which the market discounts new information. This does not imply that individual investors always correctly interpreted the company's action, but it does indicate that *on balance* the market was able to assess the chances that the split would be succeeded by other favorable news. Not only was the market's reaction unbiased; it was also fairly swift, for the implications of the split were fully reflected in the stock price by the end of the month. If this is typical of the market's reaction to public information, it does not bode well for the chance of obtaining superior performance on the basis of such information.

Chapter 6 *Listing*

In June 1963 Carter Products was restrained from issuing a nonvoting stock. In handing down his decision, the judge pointed out that the company's action would have caused its existing stock to be delisted and would therefore have damaged substantially the interests of the shareholders. Central to this argument is the assumption that an exchange quotation confers significant benefits on the stockholder.

An analysis of the behavior of stocks in the prelisting period produces a picture that is reminiscent of the price action before a split. Thus, Figure 15 indicates that new listings have been most common in buoyant markets, and the first columns of Table 13 show that the particular stocks concerned have been ones that have performed relatively well. The application for a quotation, like the decision to split, seems to have been a symptom of prosperity.

Several months normally elapse between a company's first approach to the Exchange and the actual admission to trading.

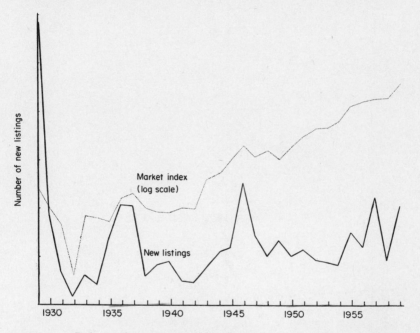

FIGURE 15. Relation between number of new listings on the New York Stock Exchange and the level of the market.

Tables 13 and 14 demonstrate that during this time the stocks experienced further abnormal gains. It is worth noting that despite the fact that formal application is normally made only with the agreement of the Exchange, the news of the approval was generally greeted with enthusiasm by the market.

These high rates of return may not be entirely an outcome of the listing application. Over-the-counter stocks are for the

TABLE 13. *Price Changes of Stocks before and after Listing*

Year	Number of Stocks	Six Months before Listing to Application Date		Application Date to Approval Date		Approval Date to Listing		Day after Listing		Month after Listing	
		Listed Stocks	DJIA*	Listed Stocks	DJIA	Listed Stocks	DJIA	Listed Stocks	DJIA	Listed Stocks	DJIA
1961	52	+10.9%	+5.7%	+7.0%	+1.5%	+6.7%	+0.8%	+0.9%	+0.1%	−2.1%	+1.1%
1962	45	− 2.2	−5.1	−1.2	−1.5	−0.5	−1.4	−0.3	+0.0	−3.7	+0.4
1963	58	+10.7	+8.0	+3.1	+1.0	+6.0	+1.5	−0.4	+0.1	−1.5	+1.4

* Dow-Jones Industrial Average.
Source: After Adams.[1]

most part riskier investments and are held only in the expectation that they will provide their owners with above-average
returns. The stocks that are considered in Table 13 appear to
be no exception in this respect, but the very consistency with
which these issues outperformed the market implies that risk
is not the sole explanation of their behavior.

TABLE 14. *Performance of Stocks Three Months before Listing
to Date of Listing*

Number of Issues	Date of Listing	Exchange	Average Change in Stock Price	Average Change in Market Index	Percentage of Stocks Out-performing Market
94[a]	1960–1961	NYSE	+22%	+2%	72%
25[b]	1963	NYSE	+17	+7	72
52[c]	1966–1967	Amex	+24	−2	81

[a] Source: After Merjos.[98]
[b] Source: After Merjos.[99]
[c] Source: After Merjos.[97]

So far there seems little reason to doubt the correctness of
the Carter Products decision. Yet, when one turns to consider
the postlisting behavior of these stocks, a somewhat different
picture emerges. It is not possible to make completely accurate
comparisons between prices of unlisted and listed securities,
for the only guide to the former is the published list of inter-
dealer quotations, which exclude any retail markup or mark-
down. Despite this problem, it does appear that some part of
the earlier price appreciation is not maintained. Almost all
studies of early weeks of trading on an exchange have noted
this tendency,[97–99,112,147,150] and it is clearly apparent in the
sample of stocks reviewed in Table 13. An extensive analysis
of the long-term performance of all new listings on the New
York Stock Exchange between 1926 and 1965 disclosed that

the rate of return on these issues was somewhat inferior to that of the general market, whether measured over the following year, the following three years, or the following five years.[53] Such a reaction is intriguing, for it seems to indicate that the prelisting exposure causes the market to become oversanguine. This is not the only indication that investors can be misled by publicity. Chapter 9 will demonstrate that a similar degree of optimism seems to be generated by the sale of new, unseasoned issues. Another interesting but minor example was provided by an analysis of the market's reaction to the publication of the name of the speaker at a forthcoming meeting of the New York Society of Security Analysts. Table 15 suggests that this an-

TABLE 15. *Reaction of the Stock Price to the Announcement of the Speaker at a Forthcoming Meeting of the New York Society of Security Analysts*

	Number of Advances	Number of Declines
Two weeks before meeting	76	44
Two weeks after meeting	51	73

Source: After Merjos.[100]

nouncement encouraged expectations that were not subsequently satisfied.

The postlisting price reaction is not the only reason for being suspicious of the claim that investors place a lasting value on exchange quotations. Some further doubts were inspired by an analysis of stocks that were traded for the first time on the New York Stock Exchange between 1960 and 1965.[56] The price of each of these issues was considered at two different dates, one approximately nine months before listing, the other approximately nine months after. This resulted in a total of nearly 400 stock prices. Multiple regression was used to explore the degree to which these prices were influenced by such factors as the prospective growth rate, its stability, and the level of dividends. Although these characteristics could explain only a relatively small part of the variations between one price and another, in each case the direction of the effect coincided with expectations. The next step was to assess whether any useful improvement in the results could be secured by considering as well the market in which the stock was traded at the time. After the impact of the other factors had been taken into account, exchange quotations did not appear to exert any significant effect on the stock price. Investors, it seems, use the same method to value both listed and unlisted securities.

This study is open to many objections. The decision to consider the stock prices themselves rather than the price-earnings ratios heightens the risk that the results may have been dominated by one or two high-priced securities. In addition, since much of the variation in stock prices was left unexplained, there is a danger that the true effect of listing may have been distorted by the omission of an additional factor to which it is indirectly related. Fortunately, however, these problems are mitigated by the fact that the pre- and postlisting prices refer to the same sample of stocks. Some available counterevidence weakens one's confidence in these findings still further. Exercises of the kind described in the introduction to Part I, which seek to explain differences in the earnings multiple in terms of factors such as the expected earnings growth, have customarily shown that there is also a relationship between the multiple and the market in which a stock is traded. Yet this result should not be taken too seriously, for it is very probable that the premium observed on listed securities was due at least in part to fundamental differences between the two groups of companies, rather than to the fact of listing itself.

Despite the limitations to the evidence, the apparent absence of any distinction between listed and unlisted issues does serve to draw attention to an alternative explanation of the prelisting rise. In addition to being a sign of recent prosperity, the application for listing may represent a tacit declaration by management that the company's success is no temporary phenomenon. The credibility of such an assertion is strengthened by the fact that the Exchange will encourage the firm to proceed with the application only when it is also convinced of the soundness of the enterprise.

In sum, the evidence presented in this chapter has suggested that companies generally apply for a stock exchange quotation only after a substantial relative improvement in their stock price. Although these gains continue after the approval date, they do not appear to be permanent, for during the subsequent weeks a rather curious reaction in the price seems to occur. Thereafter, the market apparently does not view a listed stock very differently from one that is traded over the counter, so that it is quite possible that the prelisting rise is caused not by the change in status but by the favorable earnings prospects that are thought to be associated with the change. If this is so — and the evidence is merely suggestive — a company cannot bring about a permanent, worthwhile improvement in its share price by obtaining an exchange quotation.

Part II
UNUSUAL ACTIVITY AND
THE STOCK PRICE

Although there is a widespread belief that the volume of stock market activity provides a useful guide to the future course of stock prices, such matters have received very little systematic investigation. There is some evidence to suggest that when information occurs, it comes not as "single spies" but in concentrated bursts, which are matched by a surge in dealing and by sharply fluctuating prices.[109,111] Consequently, heavy market volume tends to be accompanied by large price changes and to be followed by more heavy volume and more large price changes.[161]

Studies that have also taken account of the direction of the price movement have not been so fruitful. One such analysis indicated a tendency for heavy volume to precede a rise in stock prices and for low volume to precede a decline, but the credibility of this result is seriously impaired by the adjustments that were made in the price data.[161] Other investigations have produced no reason for believing that a high or increasing volume consistently precedes a rise or a fall in the stock price.[59,63]

Since a change in volume can be caused by a shift either in the supply or in the demand schedule, it is perhaps not surprising that variations in the level of activity do not by themselves exert any simple predictable effect on the stock price. For this reason, the following chapters concentrate on events that involve an identifiable change in the amount of stock on offer. The direct impact on the stock price of a shift in the supply curve has important implications for investor liquidity and for the marginal cost of new capital.

The discussion of these questions will suggest that an increase in the supply of stock is liable to take on added meaning according to the supposed motives of the seller. Consequently, a large portion of Part II will also be concerned with an assessment of the significance of certain kinds of unusual activity and of the market's skill in recognizing it.

Chapter 7 *Block Sales and the Secondary Distribution*

Many institutional fund managers complain that in the quest for superior performance they are seriously handicapped by the effect of their activities on the price of a stock. A dramatic demonstration of this is provided by the declines that have occurred whenever investors have tried to dispose of large quantities of stock. Consider, for example, the market's reaction to the two largest blocks ever to be sold on the floor of the New York Stock Exchange. In October 1966, following rumors of difficulties with the Xerox 2400 copier, stockholders sold 400,000 of the company's shares in three days, including an unprecedented block of 96,000 shares worth $14 million. By the end of the three days the price had fallen 32 points to $132.

Even more impressive was the activity in Control Data in August 1968. Four days after the company predicted a decline in earnings, investors sold over 900,000 shares in a single session, involving one block of 374,000 shares worth more than $50 million. The price on that day fell from 152 to $135\frac{1}{4}$.

Portfolio managers have not been the only ones to express disquiet about the effect that dealing in large blocks of stock has on prices. Many observers have feared that trading by the more wealthy and aggressive institutions causes severe price fluctuations, which are against the public interest.

Over the last few years, several people have come to question the basis for these concerns. They have pointed out that if the demand for stock can be stimulated only by large price discounts, the demand schedule must be very inelastic. Normally, this is the case when no close substitute is readily available. Thus, demand for works of art or World Series tickets is not affected much by the price because each product is almost unique. Yet it seems a little odd to suggest that the stock of a single company is likewise prized for its unique qualities. Some investors may own Xerox for sentimental reasons or because they like the color of the share certificate. Most own it because if offers the prospect of a rate of return that is adequate compensation for the risks involved. Since every other stock in the United States is held for the same reason, only a small relative decline in the price of Xerox should be sufficient to bring in many buyers who previously felt it was no more attractive than some other security. In this case, an increase in the supply of stock should have a significant effect on the price only if it is large relative to the supply of all available stocks. The situation is analogous to that of a wheat farmer, whose product is sold on the strength of qualities that it shares with the output of many other farms. As a result, he can expect to be able to sell additional quantities of wheat with merely an imperceptible effect on the price, and he is liable to depress the price only if the incremental supply is large in relation to the total amount that is for sale.

Here then is the dilemma. On the one hand, the experience of most institutional portfolio managers indicates that it is difficult to dispose of large amounts of stock without inducing a sizable decline in the price. On the other hand, the close competition between investors ought to work to equalize the attractions of individual stocks, so that it should be necessary only to offer stock at a small discount in order to stimulate demand.

One way to investigate the ability of the market to digest large offers of stock is to examine its reaction to different secondary distributions. These occur only when the block cannot be easily sold in the regular manner. Secondary distributions therefore represent substantial additions to the trading supply of a security. Since the war, the average secondary distribution has involved more than 2% of the firm's outstanding stock and has had a value of nearly $5 million. Although other means are available for the disposal of such large blocks, the secondary distribution has proved the most popular and has accounted in recent years for over 1% of New York Stock Exchange volume. This makes its effect on price a subject that is important in its own right.

The secondary is handled by a member firm, which combines with other members and nonmembers to accumulate sufficient orders to permit the disposal of the block off the floor. The sale usually takes place after hours at a price that is very close to the latest price registered on the Exchange. For this service, the seller pays a commission generally equal to twice the normal rate and the buyer pays no commission.

One can get a good picture of the immediate impact of the secondary distribution by looking at a sample of 345 such offerings made between 1961 and 1965.[129] In a number of these cases, the effect on the price of the stock is liable to have been obscured by the influence of simultaneous changes in the general level of the market. One way to adjust for these market fluctuations was described in Chapter 5. The first step is to examine how the price usually reacted to changes in the level of the market during periods that involved no secondary distribution. This estimate can then be used to judge how far the stock was affected by market movements in the days leading up to and following the offering. For example, suppose that a comparison of the action of the stock and the market in other periods suggested that each change in the market index was on the average accompanied by twice as large a change in the price of the stock. Then, if on the day of the secondary offering the index fell 1% and the stock price declined 5%, one might judge that in the absence of any market change the fall in the stock price would have been 3%. This abnormal price change should provide a better indication of the way in which investors responded to the distribution.

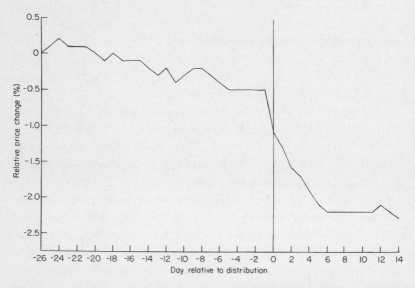

FIGURE 16. Relative performance of 345 stocks over period of distribution (after Scholes).[129]

Figure 16 depicts the average adjusted price changes of the 345 stocks during the weeks immediately before and after the offering. It is clear that the secondary distributions were typically associated with a modest fall in price. Over the entire 40-day period the stocks suffered a decline of 2.3%, the major part of which was concentrated on the day of sale and on the five succeeding days.

To see how far the cost of secondaries increases with size, a scatter diagram was constructed showing on one axis the price change on the day of distribution and on the other the value of the shares traded. This is reproduced as Figure 17.

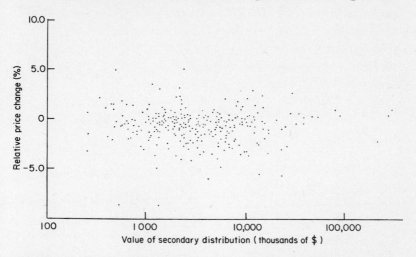

FIGURE 17. Relation between size of secondary distribution and performance on day of distribution (after Scholes).[129]

The result contrasts sharply with the popular view, for the price declined no more sharply when $100 million of stock was sold than when the figure was $100,000. The same effect is apparent if the stocks are segregated into two groups according to the value of the offering. On the day of sale stock prices fell by 0.7% when the distribution was unusually large, and in the remaining cases they fell by 0.3%. Over a period of several weeks the performance of the two groups was identical.

It could be argued that the relevant measure of size should not be the dollar value of the issue but rather the proportion of the company's stock that is involved. The analysis was therefore repeated with this modification. It made no difference. The price decline was no greater when 30% of the firm was sold than when the proportion was less than 0.1%.

As a check on these findings, it is worth looking also at the long-term effects of secondary distributions, while at the same time widening the sample to include over 1200 issues made between 1947 and 1964. Figure 18 depicts the monthly

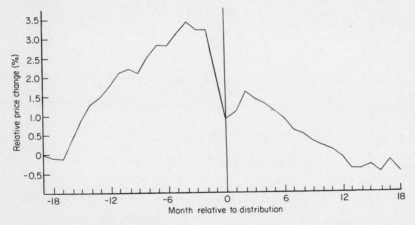

FIGURE 18. Relative performance of 1207 stocks over period of distribution (after Scholes).[129]

performance of these stocks after adjustment is made for the influence of the market. The first thing to notice is that the pressure on prices was greatest during the month of distribution. On the average, during this month there was a decline of just over 2%. To see whether the fall was more severe when a large amount of stock was involved, the size of the issue was plotted against the change in the stock price during the month of sale (Figure 19). Once again this characteristic appears to be quite unrelated to the extent of the price fall. The largest distributions were associated with a decline over the month of 2.1% and the smallest with a decline of 2.2%. Reexpressing size in terms of percentage of stock traded does not affect the conclusion.

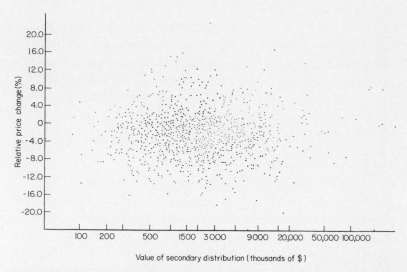

FIGURE 19. Relation between size of secondary distribution and performance in month of distribution (after Scholes).[129]

All this evidence strongly suggests that the price reaction associated with a secondary offering is not simply a consequence of the additional supply of stock. This view is reinforced by another feature of the stock's performance. If the price fall were just a matter of market indigestion, one might expect a recovery when the digestive processes were complete, but the analysis of daily data reveals no trace of such a recovery, and the monthly figures show no more than a very limited rally before the price resumed its gradual decline. It seems then that stocks are indeed close substitutes for each other and that it costs very little more to shift $100 million of stock than $100,000. But in this case, why did the stock price usually fall at the time of the secondary offering, and why did the price of Xerox or Control Data decline so sharply on the occasion of the block sale? If Figure 20 correctly rep-

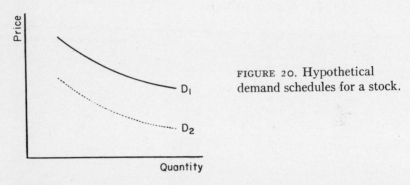

FIGURE 20. Hypothetical demand schedules for a stock.

resents the demand schedule just before the sale, a significant decline in price can take place only if the whole curve is shifted permanently downward from D_1 to D_2. This would occur if the secondary distribution coincided with the publication of bad news. It would also occur if investors interpreted the offering as a harbinger of such news and so revised downward their assessment of the stock's value. The fact that the price never recovered from its new level would fully justify such a reaction.

It may be instructive to consider in this light the market's response to different secondary distributions. Some are registered with the Securities and Exchange Commission, and a 20-day waiting period is then enforced before the sale can take place. This registration is usually optional, but when the transaction could affect the control of the company, it becomes obligatory. In either circumstance, the market might well conclude that the owner would not be taking such a step if he were in possession of important private information. Therefore, if the market reaction to an offering depends on its implications rather than its size, registered distributions should prompt an earlier but smaller decline in price. Figure 21 confirms that this was the case.

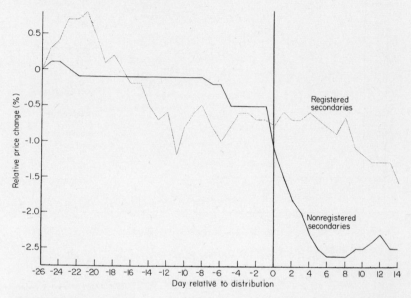

FIGURE 21. Comparison of registered and nonregistered secondaries (after Scholes).[129]

Data provided by the SEC make it possible also to categorize the performance of the stocks according to the type of seller (Figure 22). Even in the months leading up to the offering, there were substantial divergences in the price action of these groups. In particular, corporate insiders and private individuals showed a tendency to dispose of holdings that had experienced unusual appreciation. In the case of the former, this may simply follow from the exercise of stock options. In the case of the latter, it suggests that the motive for sale may have been in part the desire to prevent an imbalance in the portfolio or to devote some of the increased wealth to current consumption. Some more evidence on this question is provided in Chapter 12.

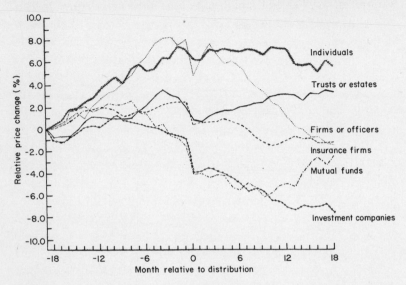

FIGURE 22. Comparison of secondaries by type of seller (after Scholes).[129]

During the actual month of distribution, the sharpest falls were experienced by stocks sold by insiders, investment companies, and mutual funds. In contrast, those sold by individuals and trust companies declined only slightly. This distinction applied not only to the month but also to the day of sale. What makes this a little surprising is that the identity of the seller is not released, except when the distribution is registered. At least two explanations are possible. It may be that insiders, investment companies, and mutual funds are more prone to sell large amounts of stock as soon as any unfavorable news appears. What may also happen quite frequently is that investors correctly guess the identity of the vendor and then react according to the amount of information they believe him to possess. It seems plausible to suppose that individuals and trusts often sell stock to satisfy a need for cash, in which case block offerings by these groups should cause very little concern. Corporate insiders, on the other hand, are always likely to be well informed, so that any indication that an insider is responsible for the secondary would understandably create some alarm. If the market did in fact reason in this way, it was in retrospect fully justified. Figure 22 demonstrates that on the average the stocks sold by individuals and trusts did not perform unusually badly. At the other extreme, offerings by insiders were followed by a prolonged decline in price. The performance of stocks sold by other institutions was less decisive. Nevertheless, in each instance the offering typically preceded some months of relatively poor price performance.

What does all this evidence show? First, it suggests that the complaint of the institutional fund manager is not without some foundation, for the large block offering does exert pressure on the price of the stock. In the case of secondary distributions, the average additional cost to the seller is almost 3%. This is not insignificant and should restrict the degree of portfolio turnover. Yet it is probably less than most investors would assume and should certainly not deter a stockholder with serious qualms about the future.

Where the portfolio manager is so often wrong is in directly attributing this decline to the size of the offering. In fact, the impact of large block sales does not seem to depend on how large the block is but on how much information it conveys. Just as the market interprets dividend increases, stock splits, and listing applications as heralding good news, so the block offering is correctly regarded as a portent of bad news. This fact in no way diminishes the task of the portfolio manager, but it does cast it in a somewhat different light. In these circumstances, trading becomes worthwhile only if the market is likely to underestimate the information on which the action is based. The problem becomes that of concealing one's enlightenment and advertising one's ignorance.

Even though this problem may be less acute for the manager of the very small fund, there is no reason to believe that the advantage is in any way critical to performance. Studies of mutual and pension funds have revealed no trace of any connection between size and performance.[8,69,135] For instance, Figure 23 shows the experience of 34 mutual funds from 1953 to

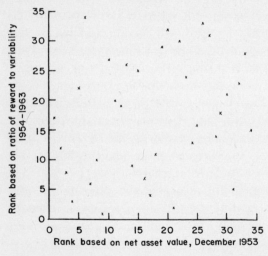

FIGURE 23. Relation between size and performance of 34 mutual funds (after Sharpe).[135]

1963. The order of the funds in terms of their 1953 market value is shown on the horizontal axis and their order in terms of subsequent performance on the vertical axis. The wide scatter of the points is testimony to the lack of any significant relationship between the two quantities.

The increase in block trading poses important problems for

the undercapitalized specialist and therefore for the whole structure of securities markets. This is incontrovertible. However, there is no evidence to suggest that the activities of large institutions are disequilibrating. If they were, they would induce purely temporary changes in stock prices. Instead, it appears that these transactions serve the economically useful function of causing prices to adjust more rapidly to available information.

It is sometimes suggested that it is unwise to purchase stock made available through a secondary offering. In the short term, there is little to support this view. The slight decline in price over the following week causes the buyer to lose approximately 1% of the value of his investment, but this is offset by the fact that he does not pay any commission for the share. Thus, there is little to choose between taking up a secondary or buying in the market one week later. What an investor should not do as a general rule is to buy in the market immediately after the offering, for then he both pays commission and suffers the short-term fall in price. If one considers the long-term price movement, there seems to be rather more justification for the view that buyers of secondaries fare relatively poorly. The price discount does not fully recognize the information possessed by the seller, and the stocks involved experience an additional 1% price decline over the following year.

The Securities and Exchange Commission has expressed some concern about the fact that the investor does not receive an opportunity for unhurried consideration of the issue except when the distribution is registered. However, the rapidity with which a block is sold and the absence of any disclosure rule do not seem to result in any great hardship for the buyer, for he appears quite competent to judge the probable motive for sale without the expensive and cumbersome process of registration.

There are some other interesting aspects to these findings.

The stocks sold by mutual funds, investment companies, banks, and insurance firms reached their lowest point approximately twelve months after the offering. There is some separate evidence to suggest that if an investor can predict earnings changes over a future period, he can more safely predict the stock's rate of return for that period than for some shorter or longer time.[82] Since security analysts tend to concentrate their efforts on forecasting company earnings a year ahead, one might expect that portfolio purchases or sales would tend to reach their most profitable point after about a year. One or two internal institutional studies have suggested that this is in fact the case, and now the record of secondary offerings provides a little additional confirmation. The question is not unimportant, for superior performance is possible only if a fund's investment policy is consistent with the analyst's forecasting horizon.

By the end of the 12-month period the stocks sold by these institutions had reached a price that was about 2% below their level at the end of the distribution month and $4\frac{1}{2}\%$ below their level at the end of the previous month. This provides some reassurance that these firms are able to distinguish overvalued securities, but it also vividly illustrates that the discount needed to sell the stock together with the 2% commission combine to rob the seller of just about all the benefit of his superior judgment. Even with the advantages of some private information, good performance is not easily won.

Chapter 8 *Rights Issues*

There is no reason to suppose that the principal conclusions of the last chapter are any less valid when the company itself is selling stock than when an individual or institution decides to do so. As long as there are close substitutes for the stock, a rights issue or a placement is likely to cause a temporary oversupply only when it is large relative to the total market value of all corporations.

This does not mean that the stock price is necessarily unaffected by such an issue. The information effect present in secondary distributions could easily apply to primary offerings as well. If the company could be sure that all the new capital would be provided by existing shareholders in proportion to their holdings, the timing of the issue would be largely irrelevant, for it would not alter the fraction of the company's profits to which each was entitled. On the other hand, if the management expects a significant proportion of the shareholders to sell their new stock or if it intends to place the issue, the timing is of some importance. Should the new issue take place when the stock is undervalued, any new stockholders will benefit at the expense of the old. Therefore, as long as management views itself as responsible primarily to the latter group, it should be led to raise new equity capital when it feels that the price of its stock cannot be sustained.

This is not the only possible significance of such an issue. Whereas the fortunes of the company are unaffected by a secondary offering, this is clearly not so in the case of primary sales. The news of an impending rights issue may frequently lead investors to revise upward their expectations for future profits, but as long as this does not always happen, forecasts of earnings per share will be reduced on the average. Therefore, the announcement of a primary issue of stock may convey both indirect information about management's evaluation of the stock and direct information about the company's prospective earnings growth.

The close analogy between primary and secondary offerings suggests that the techniques employed to analyze the latter could equally well be applied to the present problem. This has been done for a sample of 696 rights issues between 1926 and 1966.[129] The general picture is broadly similar to that encountered in the previous chapter. Over the months leading up to the issue, the stocks showed unusual price gains. This tends to support the notion that the management does seek to make the offering when the price of its stock is relatively high. During the actual month of issue, the stocks fell by an average of 0.3%, and thereafter there was little abnormal price movement in either direction. Just as in the case of secondary distributions, the price fall at the time of sale was no more severe when particularly large amounts of stock were involved, so that the market seems to experience little difficulty in absorbing the additional supply.

In this respect the results were much as expected. What at first seems surprising is that the overall price decline was so slight. However, whereas the market usually learns of a secondary distribution only just before its occurrence, the formal announcement of a rights offering will typically be made about twelve weeks before the issue date, and in many instances stockholders may have received an even earlier indication of the company's intentions. Thus, the market's reaction to the news of these offerings is probably diffused over a period of several months and is not easily disentangled from the preannouncement rise in the stock price.

It should be possible to gain some idea of the information effect by considering the behavior of the stock at the time the issues are announced. No comprehensive study of this kind is available, but there are some useful clues. For example, one analysis of 81 rights issues during 1956 and 1957 indicated that from one week before the announcement until the record date, prices declined by an average of 2.9%.[155] A similar investigation was made of investors' reactions to 61 rights issues and direct offerings during the years 1962–1965.[17] This time the stocks experienced a 1.8% relative fall in price from the four-week period before the announcement to the issue date. Both studies are likely to have understated slightly the immediate impact of the announcement, for if the stock price had been weak during any other part of this period, the company might have been induced to postpone the announcement or cancel the issue. The evidence, therefore, suggests a modest information effect that is not substantially different from the case of the secondary distribution.

To the extent that this price weakness was due to the fact

that the market had not previously realized the necessity for new capital, one would expect to find a relationship between the magnitude of the decline and the amount of dilution involved. Table 16 demonstrates that some such connection does

TABLE 16. *Relationship between Amount of Dilution Caused by Offering and Price Change at Time of Announcement*

	Price Changes Relative to Market	
	Number of Advances	Number of Declines
Immediate dilution less than 7%	16	17
Immediate dilution more than 7%	7	21

Source: After Bodenhammer.[17]

appear to exist, though it is barely significant.[17] As far as one can judge on the basis of such limited data, the need for finance causes little surprise or concern.

It was pointed out earlier that unless all stockholders are able to take up their rights, the price of the stock at the time of issue is of some importance, for it will affect the division of company ownership. This, however, does not imply that the offering price itself is of any great moment. It should make little difference to stockholders whether they receive the right to subscribe for a million shares at $2 each or 2 million shares at $1. This alters neither the valuation placed on the company nor the fraction of the company to which each stockholder is entitled. Despite this, it is still sometimes argued that it is crucial "for the management to issue the least possible number of shares to obtain a given sum of money," [22] and it is not so long since a public utilities commission insisted on a higher offering price on the grounds that this would produce additional equity capital "at no cost to the company." [86]

Because underpricing in itself does not diminish the value of the firm, there are good reasons for putting a very low price on any rights issue that is not underwritten. This is not necessarily the best policy in the case of underwritten issues, since in this instance the company in effect acquires an option to sell stock to the underwriters at the offering price. Given the underlying characteristics of the stock, the value of this option increases with the offering price. The underwriters themselves are not unaware of this obvious fact, so that it is no surprise to find on examining a sample of issues that the amount of unsold stock and the underwriter's fee are both a function of the relative offering price.[86]

Whether the additional charges are sufficient compensation is a question for which no direct evidence is available. However, it may be possible to gain more understanding of the matter by considering the valuation of the rights themselves. These are equivalent to a short-term option to buy the stock at the offering price, so that an investor will be better off holding the rights than the stock if the stock later declines below the offering price. It is in precisely these circumstances that the underwriter is likely to lose from his activities. Thus, the opportunities and risks of the rights holder are a mirror image of those of the underwriter, and the additional value that is placed on the rights should be equal to the compensation that is paid to the underwriter for accepting the risks. A small sample of British rights issues was examined in this light. In the United Kingdom the issuing house bears the responsibility for managing the issue but usually transfers the risks of a failed issue to a subunderwriter in return for a fixed fee of $1\frac{1}{4}\%$. If the market values the subunderwriter's services as highly as the issuing house does, it should cost investors $1\frac{1}{4}\%$ more to acquire stock by purchasing rights on their first day of trading than to buy the stock itself. In fact, the additional cost of buying the rights averaged only 0.35%, and on only 5% of the occasions was it as high as $1\frac{1}{4}\%$. These figures were also adjusted to compensate for the difference in transaction costs, which causes rights to be more valuable than the stock even at the end of the subscription period. On this basis, investors appeared to be paying only 0.09% for the option element.

The behavior of rights over the subscription period has been a source of considerable discussion. The subject is of some relevance to stockholders who do not wish to take up their rights and are faced, therefore, with the decision of when to sell. In principle, one might doubt whether any serious variations in the price are likely to occur during such a short period, but in any case the controversy has assumed a form that robs the answers of any useful content. Instead of considering the average rate of return over the subscription period, most investigators have sought to determine the point at which the rights attain their highest price. As the examples in Table 17 illustrate, there is a strong tendency for this point to occur either toward the beginning or toward the end of the period. This is a much less exciting discovery than it may seem at first, for regardless of whether the price moves up or down during this time, its

TABLE 17. *Point during Subscription Period at Which the Rights Price Reached Its Maximum*

	1913–1925[a]		1950–1961[b]		1956–1957[c]		1966[d]	
	No.	%	No.	%	No.	%	No.	%
First third	101	47	251	54	13	46	14	67
Second third	71	33	51	11	2	8	0	0
Final third	43	20	167	36	13	46	7	33

Note: Inconclusive instances are omitted.
[a] Source: After Beckman.[12]
[b] Source: After Sarachman.[128]
[c] Source: After Leffler.[87]
[d] Source: After Soldofsky and Johnson.[140]

level halfway through the period is likely to be somewhere between its beginning and ending value. This does not mean that it is inadvisable to sell rights at this point. Even the somewhat less pronounced difference between the first and third periods is of little interest, for the distribution of changes in the rights price will tend to be highly skewed. In view of the slight weakening of the stock price during the issue month, it is not unlikely that on the average the rights do decline in value over the subscription period, but it seems most improbable that the effect is of any practical significance.

Chapter 9 New Issues

The fact that rights issues were not on the average followed by unusually high rates of return constitutes encouraging evidence that public companies do have access to new capital at the existing market rate. Whether smaller firms coming to the market for the first time have a similar advantage is a different question. The possibility that such an equity gap does exist coincides with the common belief that the rate of return on new, unseasoned issues is abnormally high. The underwriter may well have an incentive to recommend a relatively low offering price that will ensure goodwill among his institutional customers, and his views on the matter can be ignored only if the issuing company is willing to shop around for another underwriter.

Some impression of the postoffering performance may be gained from an analysis of 53 new issues reported in the *Commercial and Financial Chronicle* during the years 1963–1965.[120] Table 18 compares the price changes of these stocks with those of a similar number of randomly selected over-the-counter stocks. Whether one considers the position a week, a month,

TABLE 18. *Performance of 53 Stocks Issued 1963–1965*

	Friday after Offer	Fourth Friday after Offer	Year after Offer
Average appreciation of new issues	+9.9%	+8.7	+43.7
Average appreciation cf randomly selected stocks	+0.9%	+2.2	+32.5
Relative appreciation of new issues	+8.9%	+6.4	+8.5

Source: After Reilly and Hatfield.[120]

or a year after the offering makes little difference. At each stage the new issues displayed the better performance. The superiority of the new issues becomes even more marked if one examines a sample of offerings by very small firms. During the years 1957, 1959, and 1963, 643 offerings of new common stock were filed with the SEC under Regulation A. Quotations were available shortly after completion of the offering for 169 of these stocks. Only 21 of them stood at a discount, and on the average they sold 75% ahead of the issue price.[145] Approximately six months after the completion of the offer, the stocks continued to show an average relative gain of 61%. These rates of return are much higher than those recorded for the earlier sample. This may in part represent the greater compensation that investors probably require before they will purchase Regulation A issues. However, the difference may also have been accentuated by bias in the sample, for it is not unlikely that the missing quotations refer to the less successful issues.

Some more evidence on the initial performance of new issues is provided by a study of the London market during the years 1959–1963.[101] On the average, by the second day of dealing the value of newly issued stocks had risen by approximately 19% relative to the market, and the following weeks saw a further slight appreciation. The findings are set out in more detail in Table 19. There are two interesting aspects to this record. In

TABLE 19. *Approximate Immediate Relative Change in Value of Stocks Sold on the London Market, 1959–1963*

Size of Issue (thousands of £)	Placings		Offers		Tenders	
	Number	Change in Value	Number	Change in Value	Number	Change in Value
0– 99	78	+51%	24	+10%	—	—
100– 199	50	+26	27	+32	1	+ 5%
200– 299	37	+25	23	+22	3	+12
300– 399	15	+23	21	+34	5	+ 6
400–1000	10	+10	35	+21	4	+ 6
Over 1000	3	+15	19	+ 9	2	+ 6
	193	+24%	149	+16%	15	+ 4%

Source: After Merrett, Howe, and Newbould.[101]

the first place, it generally supports the earlier suggestion that the postissue gains are sharpest in the case of the smaller distributions. Second, the stocks seem to behave differently according to the method of sale. This is not the only indication that stocks sold by tender perform substantially less well in the aftermarket.[88] This finding raises some important questions about the most appropriate means for pricing new issues, for it has been argued that the relatively high rate of return from placings and public offers constitutes prima facie evidence that the issuing house is guilty of recommending to the company a price below the true value of its stock. If this is so, the firm's receipts might be increased by adopting the tender system, which removes the pricing function from the hands of the underwriter and places it in those of the market. Certainly the initial reception for a new issue on the London Exchange seems to have depended to a large extent on the adviser who handled it. However, one should be a little cautious about assuming that abnormal appreciation in the early weeks of an issue's life necessarily stems from underpricing. It is true that the underwriter's interest in a successful offering creates the temptation to recommend a low price, but it is also an inducement to engage in a more aggressive selling effort. Consequently, before reaching any conclusions as to the existence of an equity gap or the most satisfactory method of sale, it would be prudent to consider how enduring is the market's initial burst of enthusiasm.

The most extensive analysis yet done of the long-term performance of new issues considered all offerings of industrial stocks between 1923 and 1928 with a value greater than $2.5 million and all those between 1949 and 1955 with a value greater than $5 million.[142] (See Table 20.) Although several minor discrepancies have been observed in the data,[54] there is no reason to doubt the validity of the principal finding that purchasers of new issues have, with impressive regularity, fared less well than the market except over the short term.

This analysis was confined to the more substantial offerings of stock. However, the long-term performance of smaller issues can be demonstrated with the aid of the sample of Regulation A offerings referred to earlier in the chapter.[145] Quotations were available at the end of 1966 for 195 of these stocks. The majority of them had been issued in 1959 and a lesser number in 1957 and 1963. Regardless of the year of sale, by the end of

TABLE 20. *Price Changes of 135 Newly Issued Stocks Relative to Market*

Year of Issue	Number of Years after Issue				
	1	2	3	4	5
1923	− 7%	−15%	−22%	−38%	−33%
1924	− 2	−24	−31	−34	−49
1925	−15	−33	−45	−58	−67
1926	−10	−18	−23	−37	−33
1927	−15	−31	−40	−27	+ 3
1928	−28	−50	−59	−55	−43
1949	− 7	−12	−13	−13	−35
1950	−16	−24	−47	−42	−53
1951	−16	−21	−24	−20	−25
1952	−12	−26	−29	−30	−30
1953	−12	−21	−25	−30	− 6
1954	−47	−51	−44	−52	−58
1955	−28	−35	−18	−22	−17
Average	−18%	−32%	−38%	−40%	−38%

Source: After Stigler.[142]

1966 all the initial relative gains had evaporated. The investors who acquired these stocks at the issue price would on the average have achieved a rate of return that was nearly 13% per annum below that on the market index. When one recollects that this figure probably refers to the more successful of the Regulation A issues, it is apparent that investment in such stocks has proved very unrewarding.

These are important pieces of evidence in favor of the notion that the early enthusiasm for newly issued stocks is a temporary phenomenon stimulated by heavy selling pressure from the underwriting group. The reliance that investors are forced to place on the underwriter for information creates an unusual opportunity for effective publicity. Nevertheless, their susceptibility to such pressure indicates that the market does not always react to information in an unbiased fashion.

For the investor the implication is clear. As long as he can ensure that his participation is not limited to less-popular issues, he can expect to achieve worthwhile short-term gains by acquiring stock at the issue price. However, from any other than the short-term perspective, new issues deserve to be regarded with some suspicion. In particular, an investor would be wise to exercise unusual caution before buying stock in the early days of trading.

Although in principle the tender system may have much to recommend it, there is no evidence to suggest that in the United States the issuing company is badly served by its underwriters. Neither does the evidence support the suggestion of an equity gap. On the contrary, the inferior long-run rate of return from new issues implies that too much capital rather than too little has been committed to these businesses.

Chapter 10 *Published Investment Advice*

In the case of the secondary distribution or the rights offering, the market is obliged to infer the views of the seller from his actions. However, the opinions of many professional investors are published and are widely disseminated. Although no comprehensive study has been made of the market's reaction in these instances, there are some scraps of evidence that are worth considering.

It is possible to gain some impression of the short-term effect by looking at the recommendations contained in the weekly market letters of four large stock market services.[50] If repetitions of earlier advice are ignored, there were, during the first three months of 1953, 269 unequivocal recommendations to buy a stock and 76 to sell. The letters not only had a broad circulation but appeared to generate considerable interest among subscribers. On the day that the recommendations first appeared, the average trading volume of the stocks concerned was more than double the previous day's level. Even four weeks later, daily trading volume in the stocks recommended for purchase was still 40% to 50% above former levels, although activity in the stocks suggested for sale had by that stage reverted to more normal rates.

The first sign of any real difference in the action of the two groups of stocks occurred on the day before publication. On that occasion, 62% of the purchase suggestions outperformed the corresponding Standard & Poor's Index, as against 32% of the issues suggested for sale. It would appear that certain investors managed to take advantage of the advice before it was generally available. On publication day itself, there was again a divergence in the behavior of the two groups. This time, 63% of the purchase suggestions outperformed the market, as against 36% of the sale suggestions. As a result, any investor who bought or sold the stocks at the previous day's close would have made a profit by the end of publication day of about 0.5% before expenses. Some further slight adjustment took place on each of the four following days, so that by the end of the first week this profit would have increased to 1.1%. This appeared to be the end of the short-run impact of the market letters. By the close of the fourth week, the relative prices were on the average no different than they were at the end of the first week.

It is useful to compare these results with the short-term effects of the market letters of three other advisory services.[143] In the case of one service, an analysis was made of its recommendations during the years 1959–1963. For the other two the period extended from 1961–1964. All unequivocal suggestions to buy listed securities were examined, together with a selection of the less imperative advice offered by one service. The result was a sample of 264 purchase recommendations. For each stock an index was constructed of the price movement relative to the appropriate Standard & Poor's group index, the base date being the day before the issue of the market letter. The 264 series were then averaged to provide a measure of the relative profit that would have accrued to an investor who was in a position to buy equal dollar amounts of each stock the day before publication. This composite index is shown in Table 21.

TABLE 21. *Index of Relative Price Appreciation of Stocks Recommended for Purchase in Market Letters*

	−1 Day	Publi- cation Day	+1 Day	+2 Days	+3 Days	+4 Days	+5 Days	+6 Days
Index	100.0	100.7	101.0	101.0	101.3	101.3	101.5	101.6
	+7 Days	+8 Days	+9 Days	+10 Days	+11 Days	+12 Days	+13 Days	+14 Days
Index	101.5	101.5	101.6	101.6	101.6	101.5	101.4	101.4

Source: After Stoffels.[143]

The results are very similar to those of the first study. Substantially all the impact of the market letters took place within the first week after publication, and by far the largest single day's move occurred on publication day itself. None of these price changes was sufficient to offer an investor any very worthwhile short-term gain. If he had managed to purchase each of the stocks the day before publication, his maximum short-run profit would have been 1.6%, and if he had had to buy at the closing price on publication day, he could not have made more than 0.9%. A third and more cursory study of published investment advice found a more marked short-term effect, for the stocks suggested for purchase appreciated by 4%.[126] However, once again all of this improvement occurred within a week of the publication date.

None of these analyses considered whether any unusual price movement takes place after the fourth week, but other evidence on the longer-term performance of recommended stocks, although very fragmentary, suggests that if there is any additional appreciation, it is not very important. For instance, an examination of the suggestions made by four advisory services between 1956 and 1968 suggested that on the average the recommended stocks offered a 2% relative improvement in return over the following 12 months.[31] Although this result is quite plausible, there are some serious inconsistencies in the data that detract from its reliability.

Better evidence is available on the long-term behavior of stocks recommended by brokerage houses. In the 53 weeks beginning June 1960, the *Wall Street Journal* cited in its "Market Views — Analysis" section 1054 specific purchase recommendations by stockbroking firms.[33] While many issues may have been proposed more than once, and some may have been advocated with more fervor than others, such distinctions were ignored. The result was that on the average these issues appreciated over the following year by 3.6% relative to Standard & Poor's Index. It is possible, however, that this figure was inflated by one or two stocks with abnormally high rates of return, for the proportion of recommendations that outperformed the market was no greater than one might expect from wholly arbitrary selection. The finding nevertheless corresponds quite well with a survey of 360 brokerage house recommendations received by a British institution in 1966. By the end of three months, the purchase suggestions had on the average appreciated by 4.1% relative to the market. The sales suggestions had depreciated by 1.2%.

It would be foolish to lean heavily on any one of these scraps of evidence. Nevertheless, a general pattern seems to emerge which is not inconsistent with the analysis of secondary offerings. The performance of recommended stocks indicates that brokers and advisory services have some ability to predict price changes, though their margin of superiority is far narrower than is commonly supposed. A significant fraction of the value of the advice seems to be discounted on the day of publication, and a still larger proportion is discounted by the end of the first week.

Thus, even when the information is readily and cheaply available, a complete adjustment does not occur instantaneously. Just as the implications of a secondary distribution are increasingly appreciated throughout the following week, so published investment advice appears to be fully recognized only after a lag of several days. It is possible to point to other indications of the same phenomenon. For example, Table 22 shows the average reaction of a selection of stocks that announced changed dividends or earnings during the latter part of 1951 or 1955.[4] When the news was bad, the price declined for several days afterward. When the news was good, the price continued to rise for several weeks. Other kinds of economic information appear to exert a similar impact. For instance, Figure 24 shows the effect of changes in the Federal Reserve discount rate between 1952 and 1967.[153] On the day of the announcement the market fell significantly if the discount rate was increased and rose if it was lowered. Though the pattern is not completely uniform, the same tendency predominated both during the week before and during the week after the announcement. Similar evidence suggests that the reaction of the British market to the monthly trade figures begins the day before they are released and continues for a day or two after.[24] Finally, an analysis of ten-day automobile sales figures suggested that most of their impact is concentrated in the two days before publication and in the three days following.[39] Such lags are not sufficiently pronounced to offer short-term speculative

TABLE 22. *Price Behavior of Stocks Following Announcement of Changed Earnings or Dividends*

	−1 Day	Day of An- nouncement	+1 Day	+2 Days	+3 Days	+4 Days	+13 Days	+20 Days	+27 Days
Earnings increase greater than 200% (93)	100.0	100.3	101.0	101.0	101.0	100.9	101.2	102.3	101.9
Earnings increase 100–200% (88)	100.0	100.9	101.4	101.4	101.1	101.4	102.4	103.2	103.8
Dividends increased (99)	100.0	101.6	101.8	101.9	101.6	101.5	102.3	102.1	102.0
Earnings decline greater than 50% (65)	100.0	98.8	97.7	97.2	97.2	97.3	97.8	97.6	97.3
Earnings decline 25–50% (65)	100.0	99.8	99.5	98.6	98.5	98.5	98.9	99.0	99.5
Dividends reduced (14)	100.0	97.7	94.6	95.0	95.0	96.0	94.4	93.3	94.5

Note: Parentheses denote number of observations.
Source: After Ashley.[4]

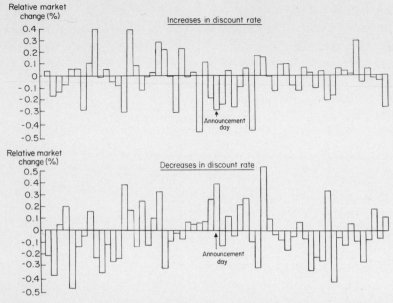

FIGURE 24. Daily market changes from 30 days before until 30 days after change in Federal Reserve discount rates (after Waud).[153]

opportunities, but they do indicate that if one must act on the basis of public information, one would do well to act rapidly.

A much more fundamental question is whether there is any point in acting at all on the basis of such information. Certainly the speed with which published investment advice is discounted poses some awkward problems for brokers. They are under an obligation not to conceal from some clients information that they disseminate to others. Yet once their views are widely known, prices are liable to adjust to a level that makes the counsel of very little value to anybody. An uncritical acceptance of the known views of the average brokerage firm or advisory service will not lead to significant gains in performance. In these circumstances, either the investor must combine information obtained from several sources to arrive at an insight that is not possessed by the rest of the market, or he must search out advisers whose opinions do not receive the respect that they deserve. In other words, it is impossible to obtain superior performance if one simply receives the same information as one's rivals. By widening one's sources of information and by systematically evaluating their usefulness, one at least creates the necessary conditions for good performance.

Chapter 11 *Insider Trading*

The picture that has evolved from the preceding chapters is that of a highly competitive capital market in which security prices adjust rapidly to reflect all generally known information. This information comprehends not only any official announcements by the company but also the published views of brokerage firms and the implied views of any large buyers or sellers of the stock.

There is no doubt that the possession of sufficiently good private information could lead to the enjoyment of great wealth. What is in question is whether any section of the community is able in practice to achieve consistently superior returns in this way. The analysis of secondary distributions managed to cast a little light on the matter. Several classes of sellers appeared to be able to foresee a decline in the stock price, but in most cases the discount that they were obliged to accept robbed them of a large part of their advantage. Only in the case of the insider was there a clear gain to the seller.

It is certainly possible also to point to particular cases where insiders have made substantial profits from private information. A notorious example was recorded by the inspector's report on trading in the Australian mining company, Tasminex. This company was incorporated in August 1969 and shortly thereafter acquired an option to take over exploration at Mount Venn in western Australia. Contrary to the geologist's advice, drilling began immediately, and on January 23 the geologist identified the presence of sulfides that could have been anomalous with nickel. That day there was unusually heavy trading in Tasminex stock, and the price rose from $2.80 to $3.30. When the market reopened on January 27, there were further sharp gains in the stock price. Later that day the company's chairman allegedly informed a reporter from the *Melbourne Sun* that Tasminex had discovered "massive nickel sulphides." This news was received in London about two hours before the close, and the shares rapidly climbed to a high of $96. The chairman's optimism did not deter him or his family interests from selling over $1 million of Tasminex stock between January 27 and 29. When the true extent of the company's discovery became apparent, the stock price reverted to $5.

Incidents such as these attract attention precisely because they are unusual. Insiders do not typically make huge profits from misleading information that they themselves have propagated, and major company announcements do not generally appear to be preceded by heavy insider buying or selling.[42] Nevertheless, company officers are well equipped to evaluate their own stock, and it seems reasonable to suppose that this fact is reflected in their investment performance.

There is a further reason for examining insider activity. All such transactions involving a hundred or more shares are filed with the Stock Exchange shortly after the end of the month and are then available for inspection by the public. Approximately one month later, a complete record of the transactions is published for all listed companies in the *Official Summary of Stock Reports*. If insiders do possess forecasting skills, then consultation of this monthly report may provide the market with useful information about the stock's prospects.

The greatest advantage enjoyed by insiders is in their intimate knowledge of the characteristics peculiar to their own firm, but it is also possible that management may become aware of changes in the general level of industrial activity or in the margin of profit more rapidly than the investment community. In these circumstances, the total amount of insider activity in any month should bear some relation to subsequent changes in the level of the market as a whole. Therefore, before investigating the significance of unusual insider activity involving stocks of a particular company, it may be worthwhile to consider briefly the implications of the total volume of insider trading. To this end an analysis was made of insider trading between 1935 and 1960 in the 30 stocks composing the Dow-Jones Average.[65] Each month a company's management was classified as either optimistic or pessimistic, according to whether the number of insiders buying stock exceeded the number that were selling. An index of the general degree of insider optimism was then constructed from the proportion of companies whose managements were optimistic. Various smoothed versions of this index were compared with the level of the Dow-Jones Average relative to its twenty-five-year trend. (See Figure 25.) A high degree of optimism tended both to follow and to precede an unusually high level of stock prices. From this fact alone it is difficult to tell whether insider purchases occurred primarily before the market rose or after, but a more

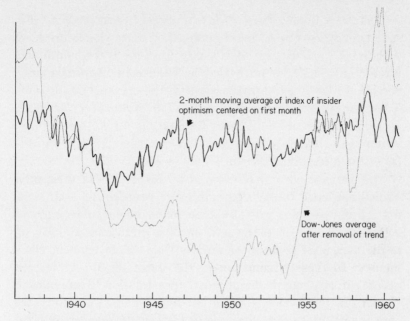

FIGURE 25. Relation between insider sentiment and market changes (after Hamada).[65]

detailed analysis of the turning points in the two indexes suggested that insider opinion tended to lead the Dow by several months.

Although insiders appear from this analysis to have only a weak advantage in forecasting market movements, they are frequently alleged to possess a clear superiority in predicting the fortunes of their own particular stocks. One simple test of this theory is to consider whether the insider's average selling price is higher than his average buying price. Such an analysis was made of insider activity in 50 stocks during the years 1957–1961.[160] As no record is available for this period of the actual days on which transactions took place, it had to be assumed that all purchases and sales were made at the average price for the month in question. On this basis insiders appeared to have purchased stocks at a price of $37 and to have sold them at $54. This is certainly encouraging evidence for the popular view, but one should not be blind to some dangers in the method. For example, the difference in prices may not indicate prescience so much as a tendency for insiders to sell heavily after a stock has risen. Another problem arises from the process of lumping together transactions in high- and low-priced stocks. The difference between the average buying and selling prices could demonstrate no more than a predominance of buying in the case of the lower-priced issues.

Two other criticisms of this approach may be made. In the first place, a large number of insider purchases involve the exercise of options. Not only does this activity show a strong seasonal tendency, but it is possible that options are generally taken up when the holder believes that the existing price level cannot be maintained. For this reason, purchases by means of stock options will be ignored during the remainder of this chapter.

It may also be argued that the total number of shares traded in each month may be a poor guide to the expectations of insiders. Their resources vary greatly, and principal shareholders of more than 10% of the outstanding stock generally deal in much larger amounts than do the company officers. The total volume of activity is therefore quite likely to be dominated in any month by the actions of just one insider who may not be the best informed and who may not even have dealt for speculative reasons. If this is so, the number of insiders who are active may be more meaningful than the total volume of insider transactions.

These criticisms do not apply to an analysis of trading in 98 randomly selected stocks during the years 1957–1960.[122] During this period there were 162 occasions on which there was an excess of at least two buyers and 210 on which there was an

TABLE 23. *Six-Month Performance of Stocks after a Majority of at Least Two Insiders Had Bought or Sold, 1957–1960*

	Price Changes Relative to Market	
	Number of Advances	Number of Declines
Majority of at least two buyers	108	54
Majority of at least two sellers	98	112

Source: After Rogoff.[122]

excess of at least two sellers. Table 23 shows the number of times that the price experienced a relative advance or decline from the mid-month level. Over the following six months, stocks bought by insiders outpaced the market twice as frequently as they lagged behind it. In contrast, sales of the stock generally preceded a relative decline.

As a check on these findings, the exercise was repeated for a sample of NYSE companies during 1963 and 1964, except that only months when insiders were both buying and selling were considered.[93] Since in 1963 the *Official Summary of Stock Reports* began to list the actual day that each transaction was made, it was in this case possible to make a more accurate assessment of insider performance. Table 24 shows that ap-

TABLE 24. *Six-Month Performance of Stocks after a Majority of at Least Two Insiders Had Bought or Sold, 1963–1964*

	Price Changes Relative to Market	
	Number of Advances	Number of Declines
Majority of at least two buyers	36	19
Majority of at least two sellers	43	81

Source: After Lorie and Niederhoffer.[93]

proximately two-thirds both of purchases and of sales were successful.

From the evidence so far, it seems clear that there are important advantages to being an insider. What none of these analyses has investigated is whether the knowledge available to insiders is fully reflected in the stock price as soon as the details of insider activity become available. The earliest point at which an investor can ascertain complete insider trading data is shortly after the end of the month. It is therefore worth considering what would have happened to an investor who at that time purchased any stock that had been bought in the previous month by an excess of two or more insiders and who at the same time disposed of any stock that had been sold in the previous month by an excess of at least two insiders. This

TABLE 25. *Six-Month Performance of Stocks after a Majority of at Least Two Insiders Had Bought or Sold, 1963–1964, Measured from Six Trading Days after End of Month*

	Price Changes Relative to Market	
	Number of Advances	Number of Declines
Majority of at least two buyers	34	21
Majority of at least two sellers	45	79

Source: After Lorie and Niederhoffer.[93]

calculation was made for the 1963–1964 sample of stocks. Table 25 demonstrates that an investor who had acted in this manner would have fared little worse than the insiders themselves.

It would appear from this that the record of insider activity contains information of value to the industrious investor. In order to assess just how great is this value and how rapidly it evaporates, a study was made of 52,000 insider transactions in about 800 NYSE stocks between 1960 and 1966.[117] This time, insiders were regarded as optimistic whenever three or more made cash purchases and none sold. Similarly, they were treated as pessimistic whenever three or more sold stock and none bought. Since heavy insider buying or selling has a tendency to persist for several months,[93] repeated indications of unusual activity may be less significant than its first occurrence. These repetitions were excluded, leaving for analysis 211 cases of insider optimism and 272 cases of pessimism.

Although the exact date of transaction is not available for the first part of this period, it should be possible to obtain some guide to the experience of the insiders themselves by looking at the performance of the stocks relative to their price at the end of the month in question. (See Figure 26.) On the average,

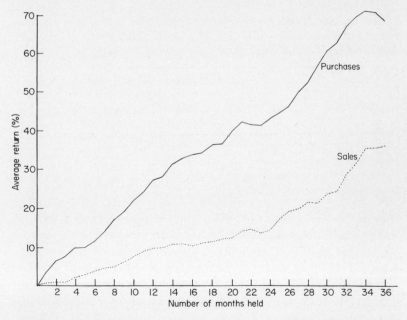

FIGURE 26. Performance of stocks experiencing unusual insider activity — no lag (after Pratt and DeVere).[117]

the stocks bought predominantly by insiders rose by 27.1% over the following year, whereas those sold rose by only 9.6%.

Only a small portion of the transactions are actually reported to the SEC by the end of the month in which they take place, so there is little chance at that point for any other investor to take advantage of the insider's foresight. However, there would be ample opportunity over the next month for an investor to respond to these demonstrations of insider optimism or pessi-

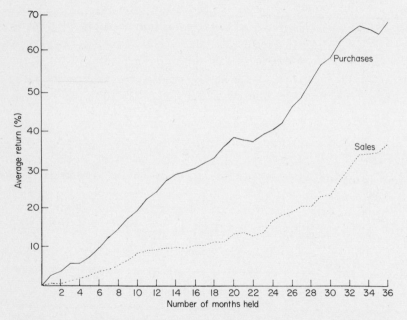

FIGURE 27. Performance of stocks experiencing unusual insider activity — one-month lag (after Pratt and DeVere).[117]

mism. Figure 27 therefore shows the performance of the two groups of stocks after the end of the following month. At this stage, very little of the advantage possessed by the insiders had been lost.

Finally, Figure 28 depicts the average performance of these

stocks relative to their level two months after the end of the month in which the unusual insider activity occurred. By this time, an investor would have had two weeks in which to study the contents of the *Official Summary*. Despite the publication of this report, and despite its lack of currency, there was still a substantial difference between the average returns of the two groups of stocks.

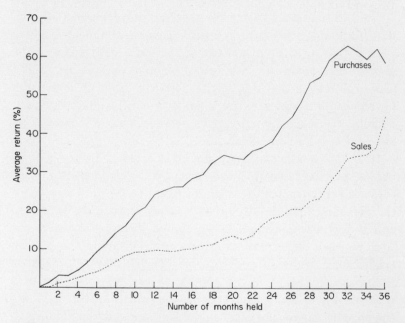

FIGURE 28. Performance of stocks experiencing unusual insider activity — two-month lag (after Pratt and DeVere).[117]

One's first reaction is that these results are a little too good to be true. However, the study on which they are based is comprehensive and detailed. The supporting evidence confirms that the rates of return from the two groups were subject to a similar degree of variability and that the difference in performance was broadly based. Furthermore, the profits made by these insiders are quite consistent with the findings of other studies of insider trading[58,93] and with the analysis of secondary distributions by insiders.[129] It is difficult, therefore, not to accept the conclusion that company officers display considerable foresight when trading their own stocks and that many of the benefits of this foresight can be captured by an investor who follows in the insider's footsteps.

Two other aspects of insider trading are of interest. In the first place, there are some plausible general arguments for expecting that a larger proportion of insider purchases than of insider sales would be made for speculative reasons. An officer who profits from his company's prosperity is much less liable to criticism than one who takes advantage of its adversities. On balance, the studies cited in this chapter tend to support this view, but it is far from clear-cut.

It is also sometimes suggested that insiders in some companies are consistently more successful at forecasting than those in other companies. This is likely to be the case where the company publishes relatively little information about its activities or where it adopts a permissive attitude toward insider trading. Such differences could also reflect simply the precise criteria that are employed for measuring insider optimism or pessimism. For example, the number of insiders typically varies with the size of firm. Therefore, as one might expect, it is less common for the insiders of a large firm to display unanimity in their actions, and it is more significant when they do.[117]

In order to determine whether insiders in some companies are persistently more successful than their rivals, an analysis was made of the record of insiders in two different periods. The first column of Table 26 shows the percentage of occasions between 1957 and 1960 that unusual insider activity proved a guide to the subsequent performance of the stock of 30 companies. The second column repeats this exercise for the follow-

TABLE 26. *Percentage of Successful Insider Forecasts*

Company	1957–1960	1961–1964
Am WatWks	83%	29%
Sears Ro	81	50
Am Airlin	76	58
Gen Elec	74	46
WhteMot	72	59
GnCable	70	71
Gen Am	68	65
GenDynam	68	59
Dover Cp	67	31
Am News	65	33
SDiegoG	65	93
Echo	64	54
Ga Pac	62	55
Talcott	61	67
UnivAm	61	64
GenTire	48	54
Sunray Oil	48	38
Nat Distil	47	68
Sbd World Air	47	56
Com Credit	47	27
MinnEntrp	44	50
Phill Pet	44	44
AmInvest	44	31
Van Raalte	43	60
Twen Cent	39	62
KimbClk	38	72
IntT&T	36	57
Starrett	35	50
Heller	29	36
Am Precisn	22	67

Source: After Lorie and Niederhoffer.[93]

ing three years. There is no correspondence between the ratios in the two periods.

The insiders whose record has just been outlined seem to constitute a rare example of an important body of investors who are well enough endowed with private information to be able to achieve consistently superior performance. What is perhaps more interesting is that any investor could have obtained a large part of the advantages possessed by insiders simply by acting on the basis of information provided by the *Official Summary*. Any widespread exploitation of this opportunity would lead to its disappearance. However, the wider significance of this finding lies in its implications for market efficiency. The failure of the market to discount the information contained in the *Official Summary* must either be dismissed as an isolated anomaly or recognized as evidence that seemingly public information can on occasion be ignored if it is not easily digested and interpreted. It could well be that the greatest opportunities for superior investment performance lie not in the rare insight or in the quest for confidential information but in the painstaking analysis of generally available but neglected sources.

Chapter 12 *Odd Lot Trading*

Failing a man who is always right, no person can contribute more to an organization than one who is known to be invariably wrong. The odd lotter, according to popular superstition, is just such a man. On this view, an assured route to investment success is to ascertain the recent actions of odd lotters and then do the opposite.

It is tempting to dismiss the odd lot theory out of hand. Yet, if one is willing to admit that certain investors consistently achieve superior performance, one is also obliged to concede that others must consistently experience below-average gains. The most likely candidate for this unenviable position is the amateur investor, for he has neither the skill nor the resources to match the efforts of the professional. The difficulty with this argument is the fact that the nonprofessional investor accounts for approximately 60% of stock exchange activity and the odd lotter alone accounts for about 10%. Unless the gains by the professional are very much larger than most studies of the subject have suggested, the performance of the odd lot trader cannot over the long run fall too far short of the average. Moreover, the absence of any simple pattern to stock price movements is indirect evidence that competition between institutions is sufficiently intense that even an unskilled investor can expect to pay or receive a fair price for his stock. Finally, it is worth bearing in mind that even if odd lotters do tend to make poor investment decisions, information about their activities may arrive too late to be of value.

If the odd lot theory is correct, one would expect to find that an unusually high proportion of odd lot sales tends to be associated with a low level of stock prices. By the same token, a particularly low ratio of sales should be accompanied by high stock prices. The upper half of Figure 29 illustrates a method of identifying occasions on which there was an unusual concentration of buying or selling in a particular stock.[146] Each point on this diagram denotes the weekly ratio of odd lot sales to purchases of Alcoa between 1965 and 1967. A trend line has been passed through these points, and around the trend line a band has been drawn just wide enough to encompass three-quarters of the points. Whenever the sales-purchase ratio falls outside this band, one may conclude that odd lotters were unusually bullish or bearish about Alcoa.

The lower half of Figure 29 shows the price performance of the stock over the same period. Here also a trend line has been used, but for present purposes the only parts of this graph that are of interest are those that show the level of the stock price during the weeks of heavy odd lot buying or selling. These have been marked with an asterisk. In this case, there was a pronounced tendency for a preponderance of buying to coincide with a relatively low price and for a preponderance of selling to coincide with a price that was above trend. This result is the reverse of that suggested by the odd lot theory.

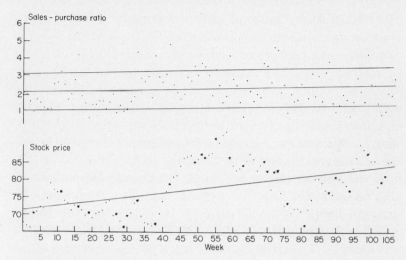

FIGURE 29. Weekly odd lot sales-purchase ratio and stock price for Alcoa, March 1965–April 1967 (courtesy of Mr. John McNeel).

The analysis was extended to 74 other stocks with similar results. In the case of 59 of the issues, decisive odd lot buying or selling proved to be more often justified than not. The total number of correct decisions was 1343. The number of wrong decisions was 563. This exercise was repeated twice. On each occasion the sales-purchase ratio was required to be further away from the trend before it was treated as decisive. The conclusions were not affected. Approximately three-quarters of the odd lotter's decisions still appeared to reflect good judgment.

It seems as if the odd lot trader is not the helpless prey of the professional but is instead an extremely astute and successful investor. Such a conclusion is even less easy to accept than its opposite. What advantage does the odd lotter possess that his judgment should be so accurate, and who are the investors making consistently wrong decisions? These are awkward questions, so much so that it is worth going back over the analysis to check for possible flaws.

The critical step in the procedure is the classification of each decision as good or bad. In the case of the early weeks the approach is unexceptionable, for the success of any action is judged according to whether the stock price was at the time above or below a trend line fitted to prices over the following two years. In contrast, decisions made in the later weeks are appraised in the light of a trend line that has been fitted to prices occurring for the most part before the date of the decision. In these cases, the analysis is seeking to do the impossible, to determine the merits of an investment action without any reference to subsequent performance. As a result, the findings are open to two interpretations. They may indicate skilled judgment on the part of the odd lotter, or they may only reflect a tendency for the odd lotter to buy a stock when its price is low relative to former levels and to sell it when the price is historically high. The latter explanation is certainly a plausible one. If the price appreciates more rapidly than it has done in the past, the odd lotter is likely to find himself unexpectedly wealthy. In such circumstances, it would be natural for him to devote a portion of this windfall to improving his current standard of living.[15] Some indirect evidence that individuals do behave in this way was provided in Chapter 7. Secondary offers of stock by private investors were typically made after a sharp rise in the stock price.

An analysis of odd lot activity in ten prewar years sheds a more direct light on the problem.[67] Each month from 1928 to 1938 the aggregate net purchases by odd lotters were compared with the movement of a market index in the preceding months. The findings are shown in the first four columns of

Table 27. For example, it is apparent that there was only one occasion on which odd lotters acquired more than 5 million shares. This huge bout of purchasing followed a severe market decline. The remaining rows of the table demonstrate that this was only an extreme instance of a common phenomenon. With impressive consistency, odd lotters acquired stock after a decline in the market and sold it after a rise.

TABLE 27. *Odd Lotter Performance, 1928–1938*

Net Purchases (thousands of shares)	Number of Occurrences	Percentage Market Change			
		From Three Months Earlier	From Previous Month	Until Following Month	Until Three Months Following
Greater than 5000	1	−67.0%	−51.0%	+3.0%	+14.0%
2000– 5000	6	−13.6	−16.5	−19.3	−20.7
1000– 2000	19	−10.6	−2.4	−3.9	−10.1
500– 1000	25	−3.4	−1.1	−3.4	−7.4
250– 500	18	+1.6	+1.4	+0.1	−2.7
100– 250	6	+2.5	+1.9	+0.8	+2.5
0– 100	10	−5.3	−1.7	+1.7	+5.8
0– −100	11	+0.6	+2.2	+1.9	−6.9
−100– −250	12	+5.4	+4.0	+3.7	+7.0
−250– −500	11	+2.3	+4.2	+2.4	+5.8
−50– −1000	8	+6.5	+3.8	+6.0	+10.8
Less than −1000	2	+6.0	+8.8	+13.6	+23.9

Source: After Hardy.[67] Copyright© 1939 by the Brookings Institution. Adapted by permission.

The final columns of Table 27 show the results of this activity. For the most part, heavy odd lot buying immediately preceded a decline in stock prices, and heavy selling took place before a rise. In fact, over the period 1920 to 1938 the average level of the market during months of net buying was 14% higher than it was during months of net selling. Such figures help to corroborate the popular view of the odd lotter. The prewar period, however, was an unusual one in a number of respects. In particular, there was a tendency, perhaps coincidental, for short-run market moves to repeat themselves. In such a situation, a policy of buying stock after a market decline or selling it after a rise would inevitably appear foolish. What is needed is some more evidence as to how odd lotters have fared in recent years.

TABLE 28. *Odd Lotter Performance, 1965–1969*

Net Purchases (thousands of shares)	Number of Occurrences	Percentage Market Change	
		From Three Months Earlier	Until Three Months Following
Greater than 2500	3	−2.0%	+2.8%
2000– 2500	2	−5.2	+1.5
1500– 2000	1	−13.5	+6.9
1000– 1500	6	−1.0	+0.6
500– 1000	5	−4.8	−3.3
0– 500	6	+0.6	+1.3
−500– 0	8	+2.0	+1.5
−1000– −500	6	−0.0	+0.4
−1500– −1000	7	+0.1	−1.4
−2000– −1500	5	+7.5	+1.5
−2500– −2000	7	+2.6	+2.3
−3000– −2500	1	−1.3	+12.7
−3500– −3000	2	+6.9	+4.7
−4000– −3500	3	+3.4	−1.2
Less than −4000	1	+0.8	−0.8

For this purpose, the preceding exercise was repeated in an abbreviated form for the years 1965–1969. (See Table 28.) Again the first portion of the table indicates that the individual investor tends to sell off some part of his portfolio after any unusual increase in its value. This time, however, there is no obvious tendency for odd lot sales to herald an unusual rise in the market level.

This approach considers only the private investor's ability to predict short-term market changes. It takes no account of his success in distinguishing among stocks. It is possible to obtain a little insight into this subject by looking at the records of the two dominant odd lot dealers for the years 1955–1962.[84] From these, one may distinguish the 20 stocks that were bought most actively by odd lotters and those that were sold most actively in each month. The first two columns of Table 29 provide

TABLE 29. *Returns from Odd Lot and Round Lot Trading, 1955–1962*

Holding Period	Most Active Odd Lot Purchases	Most Active Odd Lot Sales	Most Active Round Lot Stocks	Dow-Jones Average	Standard & Poor's Composite Index
6 months	6.2%	7.2%	4.3%	5.7%	6.3%
1 year	11.1	11.9	7.8	10.3	11.0
2 years	19.0	19.4	11.1	19.4	20.4

Source: After Klein.[84]

a comparison of the rates of return that were subsequently offered by these two groups of stocks. Regardless of the period over which the returns are measured, the issues that the odd lotter bought most aggressively appreciated less than those that he sold. Once again the evidence seems to bear out the theory.

When two groups of stocks have consistently different rates of return, it is common to find that the better-performing issues have the disadvantage of being riskier, but in the present case the stocks bought by the odd lotters were slightly more volatile than the ones they sold. It is difficult, therefore, to argue that the odd lotters were merely trading greater appreciation for increased security.

There is one disturbing aspect to these findings. The final column of Table 29 demonstrates that the rate of return on odd lot purchases, though lower than that on sales, was still comparable to that on the Dow-Jones and Standard & Poor's indexes and was considerably greater than the return on the 20 most actively traded round lot stocks. Not all these differences can be explained in terms of the riskiness of the stocks concerned. Neither is it plausible to suppose that despite the inability of odd lotters to distinguish among stocks, everything they touch turns to gold. It seems likely, therefore, that the divergence between the performance of stocks traded by round and odd lotters is in large part fortuitous. In this case, the much smaller difference between the performance of odd lot purchases and sales could also be coincidental.

Although the evidence continues to be far weaker than one might wish, the odd lotter does emerge from these studies as unsuccessful both in timing his investments and in selecting individual securities. However, this digression into specific aspects of odd lot trading was originally prompted only by the difficulty of interpreting the earlier attempt to assess his overall performance. To this wider subject it is now necessary to return.

A simple way to assess an investor's performance is to keep a periodic tally of the amount of realized and unrealized profits on his recent transactions. Just such an analysis has been made of odd lot activity in 16 different stocks during the period 1965 to 1967.[73] It was assumed that each week's transactions were effected at the Friday closing price and that the odd lotter paid neither commissions nor taxes. The profitability of each quarter's activity was then evaluated at the end of that quarter. The average outcome of each period's trading proved to be a sizable dollar loss. An objection to this calculation is that it measured the odd lotter's performance over a very short time span. This may not be too serious, since the major distinction between the professional and the odd lotter is likely to be that the former can react more swiftly and accurately to unexpected events. Nevertheless, in order to see whether the losses persisted over the longer term, each transaction was evaluated at the end of the three-year period. Once again the odd lotter was revealed as suffering substantial losses. Here then is some further support for the popular view of the odd lotter, although the evidence is still by no means conclusive. The period of time and the selection of issues are both far too small for that to be the case. Nor is the skeptic entirely without grounds. An analysis of odd lot activity in 75 stocks during a brief 18-month period beginning in February 1965 was unable to find any significant association between the odd lot sales-purchase ratio in one week and the change in the price of the stock during the subsequent four weeks.[80]

It may be possible to gain further insight into the fortunes of odd lotters by concentrating on the times when they change from being net buyers to being net sellers. If these switches are an indication that professional investors have begun to acquire stock, they might herald an unusual rise in price. In the same way, a switch on the part of odd lotters from being net sellers to being net buyers may signal that the stock is about to decline in price and should be sold. In practice, the sales-purchase ratio for individual issues is liable to vary quite erratically from week to week, so that an investor who followed such a precept would be engaged in almost continual activity. This difficulty would be avoided if he bought stock only when a four-week average of the sales-purchase ratio moved above 1 and sold it only when the moving average fell below 1.[80] Assume that an investor had employed such a rule to determine his actions in 75 stocks throughout an 18-month period beginning March 1965. On the average, he would have found that a stock rose in price by 0.14% following a purchase signal and that it declined in price by 0.60% after it was sold. Even if one accepts that odd lotters are at a disadvantage, it seems doubtful that this rule could produce even these profits over the long term. Because odd lotters are in the main net purchasers, the sales-purchase ratio is likely to remain above 1 for the greater part of the time. Thus an investor following such a precept could expect to be short of the market more often than he was long. This is a dangerous policy.

In view of this objection, it might be more efficient to identify shifts in odd lotter sentiment by major changes in the sales-purchase ratio, although there is considerable room for disagreement as to what constitutes a major change. One apparently arbitrary approach might be to buy a stock whenever the four-week moving average of the sales-purchase ratio increases by at least 50% and to sell it when the ratio declines by at least 40%.[81] For a sample of 57 stocks, this rule would have given 30 buy signals and 13 sell signals between October 1964 and December 1967. The subsequent performance of these stocks is shown in Table 30, and the results appear to

TABLE 30. *Returns from Decision Rule Based on Changes in Odd Lot Sale-Purchase Ratio, 1964–1967*

Holding Period	Price Change of Purchases	Price Change of Sales
4 weeks	+ 7.1%	+ 3.5%
12 weeks	+13.7	+10.6
26 weeks	+28.2	+ 9.3

Source: After Kewley and Stevenson.[81]

provide dramatic support for the odd lot theory, but once again a closer look indicates that they are less significant than at first sight. A substantial part of the profit can be attributed to the fact that within a month 4 signals were received to buy the same stock. Nevertheless, this does not constitute the whole explanation. Nor do the profits disappear completely with modifications to the rule.

Many technical analysts have argued that the opinions of the odd lotter are most clearly revealed in his readiness to go short. For this reason an analysis was made of the relation between the odd lot short sales ratio and subsequent changes in a market index.[83] Table 31 demonstrates that between 1960 and 1969 a

TABLE 31. *Relation between Levels of Odd Lot Short Sales Ratio and Changes in Market Index over Subsequent Month, 1960–1969*

Short Sales Ratio	Number of Occurrences	Percentage of Occasions That Market Rose	Average Market Change
0.0–1.0	1222	56.1%	0.2%
1.0–2.0	652	71.0	1.1
2.0–3.0	181	63.0	0.4
3.0–4.0	65	67.7	1.8
4.0–5.0	43	72.1	2.3
5.0–6.0	35	88.6	3.3
Greater than 6.0	50	96.0	6.1

Source: After Kisor and Niederhoffer.[83]

large volume of odd lot short sales customarily preceded an unusual rise in price.

Not one of these studies has analyzed a sufficiently large body of data to provide significant evidence in itself. Yet taken together they offer some modest support for the view that the performance of odd lotters is detectably worse than average. As to the extent of this shortfall, one must continue to depend primarily on indirect evidence suggesting that the difference is not large. Still less do these investigations provide much help with the question as to whether an investor's performance can benefit from knowledge of recent odd lot activity. Certainly, until some further evidence is available, one must remain highly skeptical of such a possibility. In contrast to these very tentative conclusions, considerable support was obtained for the view that odd lotters typically buy stocks on weakness and sell on strength. It may be that this behavior stems from a misguided belief that it will lead to improved performance. A more convincing explanation is that it reflects the individual's attempts to achieve a balance between present and future consumption.

Chapter 13 *Short Selling*

To the investor who watched the value of his holdings shrink during the depression years, the large profits made by the short seller were particularly galling. Impassioned pleas were made for the prohibition of short selling. One author likened the practice to "a huge avaricious vulture" that "so often preys upon the all-too-dead carrion of its stock market victims," [28] while another compared it to the ghoulishness of "creatures who, at all great earthquakes and fires, spring up to rob broken homes and injured and dead humans." [52] Such purple outbursts are no longer common, but many continue to believe that short selling is against the public interest. In the United States short selling is permitted only on an uptick, and most companies are still debarred from selling short. In other countries there are more comprehensive limitations on such activity.

Many of those opposed to short selling have contended that it is disequilibrating and induces significant temporary fluctuations in the price of a stock. This view is shared by many technical analysts. However, the concern of the technician is principally with the price movements that occur after the short interest is known. It is commonly believed that as short sellers must subsequently buy the stock in order to return the shares that they have borrowed, the short interest represents a latent demand for the issue and heralds an unusual rise in price.[64] Since any rise at all in the price involves the short seller in a loss, the proponents of this theory must believe short selling to be a very unprofitable pastime. Furthermore, the argument assumes that an increase in the demand for a stock will of itself stimulate a significant rise in its price. The evidence presented in Chapter 7 suggests that this may not be the case.

Not all technical analysts behave as if short selling induces price fluctuations. Indeed, some hold that the action of the short seller helps to push the stock price toward its correct level; thus in their eyes a large short position is a bearish portent. The professional character of the short seller lends some credibility to this suggestion. Some of the most active short sellers are hedge funds. If their high management fees are employed to attract good staff, their decisions ought to be well informed. The specialist is also responsible for a large proportion of short sales. Because his trading activities usually make an important contribution to his income,[130] the stocks he sells must generally perform worse than the ones he buys.

It may be possible to answer some of these questions by looking at the movement in the aggregate level of short interest between June 1951 and June 1968. During this period the outstanding total short position on the New York Stock Exchange increased nearly tenfold to over 20 million shares. The monthly

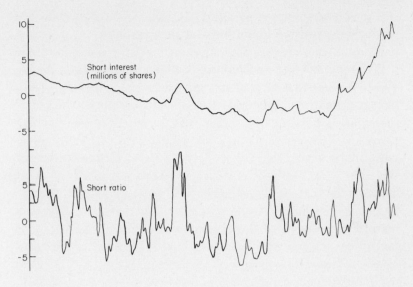

FIGURE 30. Short interest and short ratio relative to trend.

variations in the short position after adjusting for this upward trend are traced by the top line in Figure 30. It is clear that there is a close similarity between the figures in successive months; therefore a high level of short interest in one month tends to be followed by a high level in the next. This is not because individual short positions are usually left open for a long time, for SEC studies indicate that the average position is closed after about two weeks. It appears, therefore, as if the type of market situation that encourages short selling is liable to persist for several months. In these circumstances, it is doubtful whether the short interest can provide much information on market moves of less than a month's duration.

One means of assessing the relationship between the short position and the market performance is to plot both on a scatter diagram. If a high short position is associated with

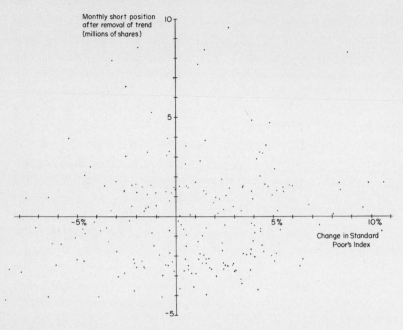

FIGURE 31. Relation between short position and market change.

rising markets, the points should lie along an upward-sloping line. If the connection is inverse, the points should cluster about a downward-sloping line. In Figure 31 the outstanding short interest after adjustment for trend has been plotted against the change in Standard & Poor's Industrial Index during the same month. No easily detectable relationship results, and the coefficient of correlation between the two series is only 0.04. This exercise was repeated with a one-month lag; thus the short position in one month was compared with the change in the market in the subsequent month. The graph was very similar in appearance to Figure 31, and the coefficient of correlation was only marginally higher. No improvement could be obtained by increasing the lag further.

It is important to note the time periods involved in this

analysis. The data for the short interest always refer to the middle of the month, though the figures are not usually published until five days later. The changes in the market index were measured on a calendar month basis. Thus, Figure 31 compared the level of short interest in the middle of the month with the index change during that month. When the market change was then made to lag a period, the short interest at the middle of one calendar month was compared with the market move during the next month. In other words, the findings imply that an investor who was uncertain at the beginning of a month whether to buy or sell common stocks would have derived no benefit from knowing whether the short interest two weeks earlier was unusually high or whether it would be so in two weeks' time. Although it would have been more satisfactory if the market performance had been measured from the day that the short interest was published, it is unlikely that the results would have been substantially different.

A second difficulty with this exercise arises from the fact that the short interest is expressed in terms of the number of shares involved. Consequently, a relatively high incidence of stock splits may create the spurious impression of increasing short interest. Since stock splits usually take place in buoyant markets, this may have imparted some bias to the results.

To ensure that these conclusions are not seriously in error, the short interest between 1962 and 1966 was adjusted roughly for the effect of stock splits.[96] Multiple regression was then employed to see whether the market level at the time the short position was announced could be explained in terms of the market level in the preceding weeks, the extent of the short position, or simply the passage of time. There was no tendency for an unusual short position to be associated either with a high or with a low market level. Neither could the short interest contribute to an understanding of the market level at any point in time after the short position was known.

Many of the fluctuations in the short position seem to be associated with simultaneous fluctuations in the general degree of market activity. This has led many observers to argue that the absolute size of the short position is less significant than its level in relation to the total trading volume. For this reason, *Barron's* publishes each month the ratio of the short interest to the average number of shares traded in the interim. As this short ratio has exhibited no more than a very gentle upward trend since 1951, the rise in short selling has kept pace only with the general increase in market activity. The variation in the short ratio after adjusting for trend is traced by the bottom line in Figure 30. Once again an unusually high or low level can be expected to last for several months, but this characteristic is less marked than in the case of the absolute size of the short position.

In order to see whether these figures have any great predictive value, they were compared with the corresponding monthly changes in Standard & Poor's Industrial Index. The coefficient of correlation between the two series was 0.15. When the short ratio was compared with the change in the index in later months, a very similar degree of association was observed. These results suggest a slight propensity for a high short ratio to be followed by an unusually large rise in stock prices, but the correlation is too weak to warrant much confidence in the conclusion.

One reason for caution is that the significance of the findings is impaired by the short ratio's tendency to take on similar values in successive months. In view of this characteristic, the direction in which the short ratio is moving is likely to be a more useful indicator of near-term price movements. A simple test of the relevance of changes in the short ratio is to consider whether the probability of a market improvement is any different after a rise in the ratio than after a fall. Between 1951 and 1968, there was a 59% probability that the market would rise if in the preceding month the short ratio had increased more rapidly than the trend. When the short ratio had declined or had risen less than the trend, the chance of a subsequent market improvement increased to 62%.

This is not the only indication that a rise in the short ratio may be a bearish signal, for between 1946 and 1965 the change in the monthly level of a market index was found to be positively related to the change in dividend payments but inversely related to the change in the short ratio during the preceding month.[66,133,134] Yet, even if one accepts this as sufficient evidence for the existence of some such association, the effect is far too weak to be of much practical value.

One further possibility remains to be explored. Short selling is typically concentrated in a very small number of issues. It would seem, therefore, that the sales are not prompted by concern about the general level of the market but rather by the belief that the particular stocks involved would perform poorly. Certainly this must be true of the large number of short positions that are used to hedge purchases of other stocks. If this is so, the implications of short selling or the effect of short covering should become much more apparent if one considers the behavior of individual securities.

One test of this possibility represents an extension of an earlier approach.[96] It was assumed that the average price of a stock during the week in which the short interest is published can be explained by three factors: the stock price in recent months, the long-term trend in the stock price, and the level of short interest. Multiple regression was used to see how well this theory could account for the prices of 14 frequently shorted NYSE issues during the period 1962 to 1966. Subsequently, an attempt was made to explain in this manner the price of the stock at various stages after the publication of the short interest. In no case was there a consistent tendency for a large short position to precede an especially high or low price level.

If it is true that the size of the short position is irrelevant to the future performance of a stock, a policy of buying securities immediately after the announcement of a large short position should be neither remarkably profitable nor unprofitable. An analysis was therefore made of the performance between October 1967 and June 1968 of a portfolio that was continuously invested in those New York Stock Exchange issues that had both large and rapidly rising short positions.[139] A similar exercise was undertaken for stocks listed on the American Exchange. The only consistent conclusion to emerge was that investors tended to sell short the more aggressive securities, so that these stocks outperformed the market when it was rising but declined more sharply when it was falling.

All this evidence has been concerned with the problem of whether it would have been possible to profit from a study of the short position after it had become public knowledge. Whether the short sellers themselves have been successful is another question. It is not, however, an easy one to answer with the aid of public information alone, for although the monthly changes in the short position are known, there is no satisfactory way to determine on what day or at what price the sales were made. One very approximate solution is to assume that all changes were made at the end of the calendar month. On this basis estimates were derived of the total return accruing to short sellers in each of 14 stocks during the years 1962–1966.[96] In almost every case, the short seller incurred a large loss. A more disturbing discovery was that these losses were not in any way reduced by the timing of the short seller's decision. In other words, the results would have been very similar if the short seller had simply tossed a coin to decide which was the best month to assume a particular short position. If this finding is both correct and typical, two conclusions follow. In the first place, short sellers must expect on the average to take a sizable loss, for given the upward trend in stock prices, the only way that they could hope to avoid such losses would be through skilled timing of their actions. Second, the fact that the variations in the short position neither add to nor subtract from the seller's proceeds makes it unlikely that they can provide any guidance to other investors.

None of the studies cited in this chapter has been sufficiently comprehensive to detect any subtle association between the volume of short selling and the price movement of the stock. Yet the absence of any pronounced tendency for prices to rise when the short position is unwound casts doubt on the suggestion that such selling is seriously disequilibrating. Neither is there any evidence to suggest that a particular pattern of short selling is a useful indicator of a stock's subsequent performance. In the eyes of one commentator, an analysis of the short interest offers "the most important single technique for determining whether a stock should be bought, held or sold." [64] This seems unquestionably to be an overstatement.

Part III
CONVERTIBLE SECURITIES

In Chapter 8, brief reference was made to the fact that a rights issue provides the shareholder with a short-term option to buy the stock. Correspondingly, the underwriter to the issue places himself in the same position as the option seller. The value of such a short-lived option is very slight, particularly when the issue price is well below the stock price, and it is by no means clear that the market recognizes that it has any worth at all.

This section returns to the subject of options and related securities. The initial chapters seek to explain the variation in the price of puts and calls and to assess the experience of the holders. Although buying and selling such options is not a common occupation, there are good reasons for dwelling on the subject. In the first place, recent proposals for a large centralized option market in Chicago could well lead to major opportunities for institutional trading in options. Furthermore, an understanding of the elements of option valuation should prove helpful when, in the later chapters, the discussion centers on the rather more intricate subject of warrants and convertible bonds. The evaluation of the former is complicated both by the fact that they are not entitled to dividends and by the fact that the investor's horizon rarely coincides with the life of the warrant. In the case of convertible bonds, the problem of valuation is made even more difficult by the attachment of the option to another security.

Chapter 14 *The Option Market*

Despite the rapid growth in option dealing, the total volume of puts and calls traded in any one year seldom exceeds 1% of the amount of stock traded on the New York Stock Exchange. Partly because of a history of unsavory practices and restrictive legislation, institutions are not active in the market. Nor have the dealers themselves done anything to encourage institutional participation. Instead, they have remained content with the high markups that are possible in an imperfect market. One consequence is that many investors remain unfamiliar with the techniques of option trading and might sympathize with the state legislator who complained that he "would not know a put or a call if he saw one coming down the aisle."

A call option gives its holder the privilege of buying a fixed number of shares from another investor within a stated period at a specified price. Conversely, a put option conveys the right to sell stock at a specified price to the other investor at any point within this period. Frequently these two options are traded in combination. A mixture of a put and a call is known as a straddle, one of two calls and a put constitutes a strap, and one of a call and two puts is a strip.

Options may be taken out for various periods of time. However, there has been a growing preference for the longer contracts which have certain tax advantages, the most popular duration being 190 days.

The price at which the option holder is entitled to buy or sell stock is customarily the same as the market price at the time the contract was first taken out. The principal exception to this occurs in the instance of 30-day options, where the contract price or striking price, as it is called, is generally open for negotiation. In all cases the striking price is liable to be revised downward during the life of the option so as to reflect any dividend payments or stock splits. In return for the right to buy or sell stock at a guaranteed price, the option buyer pays a premium, sometimes referred to as the option money. There are considerable variations in the size of this premium, but as a rough rule of thumb, the cost of a 190-day call works out at about 10 to 15% of the value of the stock concerned.

The writer or seller of an option assumes a position opposite to that of the buyer. If he has sold the call, he has guaranteed to sell on demand a fixed amount of stock at the striking price. Conversely, if he has sold the put, he has undertaken, if required, to buy the stock at the striking price. In return for this service, he receives a premium.

Options are traded not in the stock exchanges but in a separate option market in New York. Buyers obtain their contracts from specialized option dealers, who in turn arrange to acquire them from option writers in exchange for the payment of a premium. The dealer, therefore, acts as a middleman and makes his profit out of the difference between the premium he receives from the buyer and the one he pays to the writer. The fact that the dealer does not perform a market-making function in the same way as an over-the-counter dealer constitutes a severe limitation on the liquidity of the option market. In the first place, until the dealer has located an interested writer, the would-be buyer has only the vaguest indication of the price he will have to pay. Furthermore, this process of contacting a writer is liable to take several days, and even when the buyer and seller have been matched, neither has any assurance that he has obtained the best price. Finally, this cumbersome matching procedure has effectively limited the existence of any resale markets for options.

Since the option contract is always endorsed by a member of the New York Stock Exchange, the option buyer does not need to concern himself with the financial standing of the writer. The endorser, however, does require the writer to produce evidence of his ability to honor commitments. One way he can do so is by depositing margin. The minimum New York Stock Exchange margin requirements are 25% for a put and 30% for a call, though a larger percentage deposit will customarily be demanded when the writer's resources are small. As an alternative, the writer may hedge his position. Thus, by simultaneously purchasing the stock and selling a call, the writer guarantees his ability to deliver the security if required. Likewise, by shorting the stock at the same time that he sells a put, the writer confirms that he is in a position to buy the issue.

A convenient means of illustrating the nature of the option trader's position is to construct a table of the circumstances in which he stands to gain or lose money. This is done in Table

TABLE 32. *Circumstances in Which Certain Simple Strategies Are Profitable*

	Purchase of Call	Purchase of Put	Sale of Call	Sale of Put	Purchase of Stock	Short Sale of Stock
Stock price rise	+1	0	−1	0	+1	−1
Stock price fall	0	+1	0	−1	−1	+1
Premium	−1	−1	+1	+1	0	0

Source: After Kruizenga.[85]

32. The first column, for example, describes the case of the buyer of a call option. The three entries in this column denote, respectively, that he benefits from a rise in the stock price, is unaffected by a fall, and incurs the payment of a premium. The effect of any combination of these positions can be seen by adding across the rows. Thus, the buyer of a straddle simultaneously acquires a call and a put. Table 33 shows that the net result is that the owner of the straddle stands to benefit from either a rise or a fall in the price of the stock but that for this privilege he is required to pay a double premium.

This shorthand can be helpful in understanding what happens when an option writer hedges his position. Table 34, for ex-

TABLE 33. *Circumstances in Which Purchase of Straddle Is Profitable*

	Purchase of Call	+	Purchase of Put	=	Purchase of Straddle
Stock price rise	+1		0		+1
Stock price fall	0		+1		+1
Premium	−1		−1		−2

TABLE 34. *The Effect of Simultaneously Purchasing a Stock and Selling a Call*

	Purchase of Stock	+	Sale of Call	=	Sale of Put
Stock price rise	+1		−1		0
Stock price fall	−1		0		−1
Premium	0		+1		+1

ample, shows the position of a writer who has hedged the sale of a call by purchasing the stock. The effect is to convert his position from one of selling a call to one of selling a put. The term "hedging" is not, therefore, strictly appropriate. The long position ensures that the writer can always deliver stock and so protects the endorser, but it does not leave the writer in a riskless position, nor, in fact, is there any way in which he can acquire such a position as long as he is in receipt of a premium.

Just as the option writer can convert one kind of sale into another, so the buyer can similarly convert his position. Thus, Table 35 demonstrates that a strategy of simultaneously owning the stock and a put option is equivalent to the purchase of a call.

TABLE 35. *The Effect of Simultaneously Purchasing a Stock and a Put*

	Purchase of Stock	+	Purchase of Put	=	Purchase of Call
Stock price rise	+1		0		+1
Stock price fall	−1		+1		0
Premium	0		−1		−1

This conversion feature is helpful to the development of an option market. Option buyers are interested mainly in the purchase of calls, whereas writers prefer to sell puts or straddles. However, there is a limit to the extent to which this excess demand can inflate the price of calls, for there comes a point at which it pays the would-be buyer to acquire a put and to convert. The scope for arbitrage between different forms of option has led to the development of specialized conversion houses. These firms, which must be members of the New York Stock Exchange, typically buy a stock and a put while selling the call. As Table 36 shows, the net effect is a perfectly hedged

TABLE 36. *The Effect of Simultaneously Purchasing a Stock and a Put and Selling a Call*

	Purchase + of Stock	Purchase + of Put	Sale of = Call	Perfectly Hedged Position
Stock price rise	+1	0	−1	0
Stock price fall	−1	+1	0	0
Premium	0	−1	+1	0

position. The converter earns his profit from the difference between the premium he obtains from a sale of the call and the one he has to pay for the purchase of the put.

A two-way business in options may take place because the participants disagree about the expected performance of the stock. The importance of the conversion process is that it also enables trading to occur when both buyers and sellers expect the same price change yet differ in their degree of conviction or in their willingness to accept risk. It may, therefore, be useful to think of the option market primarily as a means whereby the cautious investor can transfer some of his risks to his more courageous rivals. Viewed in this light, the market is made up of three different types of participant. At one extreme is the conversion house itself. Its function is solely that of an arbitrager, and as such it assumes no risks. The converter will therefore be willing to trade in options just so long as the difference between the premium on the call exceeds that on the put by a sufficient margin to provide him with a return appropriate to a riskless investment. Typically, the converter has looked for a gross return that is $1\frac{1}{2}\%$ or more above the call loan rate.

The second group of traders consists of investors who are willing to accept some risk but not so much as that involved in holding an unhedged position in the stock. These investors may protect themselves against adverse price movements to some extent by buying a put against their holding of stock or by writing a call against it. The investor cannot usually expect this strategy to produce such a high return as a simple invest-ment in the stock, but since his position is not without some risks, he should look for a better return on his funds than the prevailing rate of interest.

The third and final group of investors includes all those who are willing to assume more risk than is involved in merely holding the stock. As long as they share the market's expecta-tion of a rise in the stock price, they are unlikely to consider buying a put or selling a call. However, they may be justified in purchasing calls or writing puts as long as these pursuits offer the expectation of unusually high rates of gain.

It seems probable that the third group of investors is the more numerous. This was the view of the SEC study, which noted that "the brokers interviewed were unanimous in the opinion that the reason most persons bought options was the opportunity it afforded them for speculation on a small amount of capital. This was borne out by the fact that when an option holder exercises a call he usually resells the stock he has acquired immediately." [131]

Because the dealer retains a portion of the premium paid by the buyer, the average outcome for all those buying and selling options must be a loss. However, it does not necessarily follow that the return from any particular form of option activity is likely to be negative. It has already been suggested that the conversion house and the investor who writes a call or buys a put to protect an existing long position may not be deterred by the realization that the probable result is a lower rate of profit than could be expected from simply holding the common stock. In contrast, those who write puts or buy calls for speculative purposes are likely to do so only if they can foresee some compensation for the risks involved. Therefore, it seems reasonable to suppose that options are priced in such a way that a policy of writing calls or buying puts is likely to produce a loss, whereas one of writing puts or buying calls is likely to produce a profit.

Whether options are in fact priced in this way will be the subject of the next chapter. In the meantime, it is worth digressing briefly to consider the reasons for the marked variation in the size of the option premium. The expected outcome from holding an option will depend in part on the return that is likely to accrue from holding the stock. Thus, the more rapidly a stock is expected to appreciate, the higher the anticipated profit from an option to buy that stock. In addition, the return from an option is likely to be greater when it is felt that the stock price could take on a wide range of possible values. The reason is that the owner of a call option stands to benefit most from the possibility of very large gains in the stock price, whereas his losses will be the same regardless of the amount by which the price falls. Thus the expected gain from a call option is a function of two factors: the expected gain in the stock price and its degree of volatility.

Since stock prices are liable to wider fluctuations over the long run, longer-dated options should command higher premiums. This dispersion of stock price changes increases roughly in proportion to the square root of the period considered, so that a stock will fluctuate $\sqrt{2}$ or 1.41 times as widely over a six-month period as over a three-month period. For this reason, the option premium should also increase with the square root of the contract's duration. The six-month option should cost 1.41 times as much as the three-month option, and the one-year option 1.41 times as much as the six-month. To see whether this is so in practice, an analysis was made of dealers' quotations on three different dates. Table 37 shows that in each case

TABLE 37. *The Effect of Duration on Call Premiums at Three Sample Dates*

	I	II	III
6-month premium divided by 90-day premium	1.34	1.32	1.35
12-month premium divided by 6-month premium	1.42	1.39	1.41

Source: After Kruizenga.[85]

the result was very close to expectation. A similar relationship seems to hold for the premiums paid to writers. The differences between these option prices are marginally less than was expected. This may partly reflect the fact that the dispersion of stock price changes does not vary exactly as suggested, but the result is also consistent with a number of investigations that have found that both buyers and sellers have achieved somewhat superior rates of return from the longer-dated options.[6,19,85] Since it costs no more to exercise a longer-term option, and since its superiority is further enhanced by the tax treatment it receives, there is a strong case for always preferring contracts of at least six months' duration.

A more complex problem is that of explaining differences in

the prices of options of similar duration. A useful start might be to examine whether these differences can be accounted for by an equation of the form

Percentage premium $= a + b \times$ expected change in stock price $+ c \times$ volatility of stock price.

Various other attributes have also been reputed to affect the price of an option. For example, it has been suggested that investors with only a limited amount of capital at their disposal will be attracted to options in low-priced stocks. Others have expressed the belief that there is likely to be a preference for options on stocks of small companies with active markets for their shares. Hence, it is worth expanding the equation to incorporate these additional characteristics. One practical difficulty in applying any such test is that there is no way of knowing precisely how much appreciation investors have expected from each stock. However, many investors do write down their forecasts of long-term earnings growth, and an amalgam of these may be used as a rough indication of the expected price growth. On this basis, the equation was fitted to data for 106 call options at the end of 1964.[95] The results were encouraging. Not only was the equation able to explain about three-quarters of the variation in the option premiums, but the expected stock price change and the stock price volatility were both shown to exert a strong positive influence on the size of the premium. Very similar results were obtained when the same equation was used to explain option prices at the end of each of the two subsequent years. These analyses also provided some support for the view that the option premium tends to be larger in the case of low-priced stocks and in the case of small companies with active markets for their stock. However, not only did these factors appear to play a very secondary role, but it is quite possible that even this weak association was merely a result of imperfect measurement of the

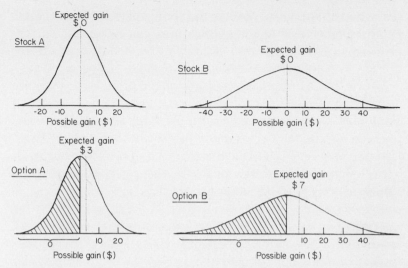

FIGURE 32. Relation between possible gains from a stock and possible gains from a call option on the stock.

volatility and expected appreciation of the underlying stocks.

A better understanding of option prices may be secured by considering the effect of holding an option rather than the stock. This is illustrated in Figure 32. The top row depicts the possible changes of two hypothetical stocks. Although both are expected to remain at their existing level, there is a much greater likelihood that the price of the second stock will move sharply up or down. The bottom section of the diagram represents the possible value of an option to buy the stock at a specific future date. If the stock price fails to rise, the option will in each case be allowed to lapse, and the holder will gain nothing. The likelihood of this outcome is denoted by the shaded area of the graph. The average of all the possible outcomes from each option is also shown. The important point to notice is that this value is completely determined by the striking price and by the possible changes in the stock price. If one also assumes that these changes conform to a normal distribution, the expected outcome from an option must depend solely on the striking price, the expected change in the stock price, and the variation in the possible stock price changes. In order to demonstrate this, an estimate was made of the profit to be expected from each of 51 options, on the assumption that the price of each stock would rise at an identical annual rate and would be characterized by the same volatility as in earlier years.[18] Despite the very crude nature of these approximations, over three-quarters of the differences in the price of the options could be explained in terms of the estimated differences in expected profits.

These exercises provide some rough assurance that the lack of uniformity in option premiums broadly reflects divergences in the market's appraisal of the stocks. With this knowledge in hand, it is time to investigate whether the general level of option prices is equally reasonable.

Chapter 15 *The Profitability of Option Trading*

One of the best-publicized studies of the effects of buying call options was undertaken by the SEC.[131] During June 1959 calls were taken out on a total of 381,000 shares. Only 43% of these options were eventually exercised, and a bare 18% of them earned a profit for their owners. On the average, the purchase of a call during that month resulted in a loss of 42 cents for each dollar invested. This experience certainly does not accord well with the suggestion that the buyer of calls is likely to require a high rate of return to compensate for the risk that he assumes. However, it is dangerous to assume that these results are typical. The decline in stock prices during the second half of 1959 may well have made this a particularly poor time to be buying calls.

The same qualification applies with rather less force to an analysis of the performance of option buyers during the period 1960–1964.[95] In this instance, an estimate was made of the effect of purchasing on January 1 of each year a six-month call option in each listed stock priced between $45 and $55 a share. The investor following such a policy would have lost 37 cents for each dollar invested. Although the result tends to reinforce the SEC findings, the skeptic can still with some justice point to the relatively stagnant character of the equity market during these months. For example, if the investor had merely held the underlying stocks for the first six months of each year, he would have achieved an average gain of only 0.2%. Perhaps a more important objection lies in the fact that the analysis was based on nominal quotations, which tend to overstate the prices that buyers are actually required to pay.

The experience of option buyers in the years 1957–1960 ought to be more typical, for during this time stock prices rose by 7% per annum, which is quite close to the long-term rate of gain. It is possible to judge the effect of holding call options during this period by examining the sales made by a single large brokerage firm.[124] A fifth of this company's business was in just ten issues. A thousand call options were sold in these stocks, giving their owners control over 118,000 shares. Despite the better market conditions, the experience of these investors was no more encouraging. Only 43% of the options were exercised, and on average the holders lost 37 cents for each dollar invested. This experience does not appear to have been confined to these particular securities, for an even smaller proportion of the call options was exercised in the case of the twenty-five most popular issues. Such findings also fit very well with the results of an analysis of 211 calls that were acquired from another broker over a fairly similar period.[19] About half of these options were permitted to expire, and their owners once again suffered a considerable loss.

It is only when one considers periods of rapidly rising stock prices that the option buyer appears to earn a respectable rate of return. The halcyon days of 1946–1956 constitute such a period. During these years a portfolio composed of equal amounts invested in each of eight leading New York Stock Exchange issues would have provided its owner with a return of over 24% per annum. In comparison, an investor who devoted an equal sum to the weekly purchase of 90-day call options on these eight issues would have realized a profit of 9 cents for every dollar invested.[85] If he had bought a succession of six-month calls, his profit would have been 35 cents on every dollar. These are substantial gains, particularly when one takes into account the rapidity with which they are achieved. Yet it is also important to bear in mind the high variation in the rates of return. This is a point of more than academic interest, for any investor who had decided in 1946 to remain fully invested in call options for the next ten years would not have made these handsome profits. Instead, he would have been impoverished on the first occasion that he was obliged to allow his options to lapse. It is also worth noting that all the profit on these options was attributable to the great bull market that began in 1953. Despite the fact that in the earlier years the underlying stocks offered a return of over 16% per annum, 90-day call options would have provided on the average a loss of 10%. Six-month call options would have given a profit of 1%.

The purchase of a call option has a hedging effect only when combined with a short position. Consequently, calls are held largely on their own or in combination with other long positions as an investment in their own right. It was this fact that led to the argument advanced in the last chapter that the holder of call options deserves a high return to compensate him for the risks involved. However, these returns do not appear to be forthcoming. Only in exceptionally buoyant markets are call options worth considering, and the profits on these occasions do not atone for the long periods of heavy loss.

Unlike calls, puts are used primarily for hedging, and their price seems to be determined by the cost of converting them into calls.[85,144] For this reason, the profitability of direct speculation in puts is of somewhat less interest. Certainly the evidence provides little justification for a policy of buying unhedged puts. The consequences of such action in strongly rising markets would have been very serious. For example, between 1946 and 1956 the holder of a 90-day option to sell each of eight leading stocks would have lost an average of 72 cents for each dollar paid out.[85] Even if one ignores the exceptional circumstances of 1953–1956, the investor in puts could still have expected to lose two-thirds of his capital on a given occasion. Some idea of the effect of holding puts in more typical market conditions can be obtained by looking at 36 actual purchases during the years 1957–1960.[19] On the average, the owners lost approximately one-third of their investment. Very similar results would have been experienced by an investor who bought 190-day puts in a selection of issues each January between 1960 and 1964.[95]

In the light of the major losses that the option buyer seems to suffer, one is tempted to feel that option writing must be a very profitable occupation. Such a view is in fact widely held. The option seller is typically a wealthier person than the buyer and usually leaves the buyer to take the initiative. It is possible that these characteristics give the seller an advantage in bargaining over the premium. A good indication of the profitability of option writing may be obtained by looking at the returns achieved by 76 writers on 851 contracts during the period April 1960 to January 1962.[78] All these writers employed the same strategy. They sold puts on margin but hedged the sale of calls. Following the same principle, they always margined the put side of straddles and hedged the call side. In each case, the effect of the writer's action was to expose him to losses in the event of a price fall, while enabling him to profit to the full extent of the premium in any other circumstances. Insofar as these writers were selling margined puts, they were exposing themselves to the risk of a considerable loss if the option was exercised. Insofar as they were selling calls against the stock, they were using the option to reduce their risk exposure. Since some of the writers were adopting a very speculative position, and since none was completely hedged against loss, one might expect that their overall rate of return would recognize this. In fact, after taking into account the losses associated with adverse stock price movements and such expenses as commissions, interest charges, and transfer taxes, the writer's return on capital was a bare 0.9%. Even on an annual basis this would have been a small reward. No allowance was made in these calculations for the fact that each of the option writers employed an agent to assist him. After paying the agent an average fee of $60 per contract, the writer's profit had disappeared completely. Of course, not all writers fared equally badly. Indeed, two-thirds of them earned more than enough profit to cover the agent's fee. Yet most of these would have been better off if they had just retained any stock that they already owned and invested the remainder of their capital in treasury bills.

Between April 1960 and January 1962 the Dow-Jones Average appreciated by 17%, so that the writer of put options could not justifiably complain that market conditions were particularly unfavorable. Certainly no other simple strategy would have been any more successful than the one adopted. The greatest dollar losses would have been incurred if the writers had followed the reverse policy of writing calls on margin while hedging their sale of puts.

To obtain additional assurance that these results are not untypical, it is worth glancing briefly at the experience of option writers in other periods. Thus an analysis of 234 options sold to dealers between 1957 and 1960[19] and one of a further 2000 options sold over the next four years[123] suggest that whatever strategy had been used, the writer would not have secured any worthwhile gains. A less detailed study has also been made of over 1000 sales of six-month call options between 1961 and 1966.[158] On the average, the losses more than outweighed any profits the writer may have made from owning the stocks.

Not all the evidence points in the same direction. For instance, when one calculates the returns that could have been made by selling six-month call options at the beginning of the years 1960–1964, option writing appears a profitable activity almost regardless of the strategy employed.[95] Since common stock prices did not advance much over this period, one would not have expected it to have been an especially favorable time for the option writer. However, it seems, quite likely that this divergent finding can be attributed to the use of nominal quotations instead of a selection of premiums actually received by option writers.

The evidence based on the experience of option writers is less clear-cut than in the case of buyers. Nevertheless, although writing does not appear to produce losses on the same scale, there is little ground for enthusiasm about either form of activity. The explanation lies in the high cost of option trading. The SEC investigation revealed that in the case of an option that was both bought and sold on the same day by members of the public, the dealer's markup averaged 21% and on occasions exceeded 50%.[131] When one also takes account of such additional expenses as agent's fees and the cost of buying or selling the stock, it is clear that the odds are weighted heavily against the option trader.

Why then do investors continue to buy and sell options? A

partial explanation can be found in the way an option is treated for tax purposes. Since it is regarded as a capital asset, an investor who is holding a worthless 190-day option can establish a short-term loss by selling it to a dealer for a nominal amount just before the six months have elapsed. Conversely, an investor who has a profit on an option can establish a long-term gain if at the end of the period he sells rather than exercises the option. This feature is particularly attractive in the case of puts, for if the investor chose instead to sell the stock short, his gain would always be deemed short-term. Yet this is not a complete answer, for an investor would need to be in a very high tax bracket before the advantage would be decisive. Moreover, if this were the only reason for buying options, there would be no demand for those of less than six months' duration.

Option trading is by no means the only speculative activity in which the average outcome for participants is a loss, and the motives of many option traders may be little different from those of the devotee of the racetrack. Each may be lured by the belief that the undertaking will prove profitable for him if not for others. The option buyer, like the gambler, is also likely to be influenced by other features of his actions. He could, for example, be compelled by the excitement of the gamble and derive positive enjoyment from the uncertainties involved. More commonly, he may be drawn by the asymmetrical distribution of the outcomes, which provides the buyer with a small chance for a very large gain against the high probability of a very small loss. Some confirmation for this last suggestion was obtained from an analysis of the circumstances in which a sample of investors decided to exercise their options.[124] It is worth noting that the option seller places himself in the opposite and presumably less welcome position, for like the fire and casualty insurance company, he accepts in return for a small chance of a large loss the high probability of a small gain.

For individuals with these unusual sets of preferences, option trading may be a rational occupation. Yet given the present structure of the market, the institutional investor would do well to shun the use of options save in the most exceptional circumstances. Such a conclusion follows directly from the inefficiencies of the present market structure, with its high cost and its low liquidity. It is, therefore, quite consistent with the belief that an active, low-cost option market could serve an important economic function. The case for some such forward market in common stocks is no different from the case for a commodity forward market. It could provide an efficient means for adjusting risk exposure and improve market liquidity. These are powerful arguments in favor of the proposal by the Chicago Board of Trade to establish a regular market in a relatively small number of put and call options with standard striking prices and maturity dates.

There are three possible advantages to such a centralized market. In the first place, the trader could more easily ascertain the price of any option without needing to go through the present cumbersome process of testing the market. Second, higher volume and a more efficient procedure for matching orders might permit a substantial reduction in the cost of option trading. Finally, it could lead to the development of a resale market for options that a trader does not wish to hold to maturity. These benefits could greatly enhance the opportunities for institutional trading in options.

One obvious function of options is to provide additional leverage. Their use for this purpose need not be limited to high-risk funds. Suppose, for example, that an endowment fund is due to receive a large increment of cash in six months' time and that the manager anticipates a sharp rise in stock prices in the interim. While it might be possible for him to borrow ahead of the cash inflow, if the Board of Trade's proposals were implemented, he could equally well take advantage of the market improvement by purchasing calls or selling puts.

Options might also be helpful in improving market liquidity. For instance, the dangers of handling large block positions in a stock could be substantially reduced if it were possible at the same time to buy puts and sell calls with the assurance that the option position could be unwound at the same time as the position in the stock.

The most exciting potential use of options is as a hedging device. Consider, for example, the two stocks portrayed in Figure 33. Both are expected to be equally sensitive at the

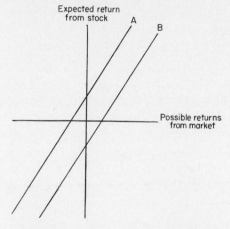

FIGURE 33. Expected returns from two hypothetical stocks under varying market conditions.

margin to any change in the overall market, but fundamental analysis indicates that regardless of the market change, A will perform better than B. If the investor simply bought A, he would be exposed to the risk of a market fall. Suppose, however, that he bought A and simultaneously bought a put and sold a call in B. If the predicted difference in the performance of the two stocks is greater than the difference between the premium for buying the put and the premium for writing the call, the investor could always expect to realize a profit, regardless of the market action. This is because any loss on A would always be matched by an even greater profit on the put option in B, and any profit on A would be accompanied by a smaller loss on the call option written on B. Thus, a fund could establish a completely protected position and make a return equal to the value of its analytical skills. If the Board of Trade plans succeed, a hedge fund would be able to hedge.

Chapter 16 *Warrants*

A warrant is nothing but a call option sold by the company. However, it does possess some important features that justify separate consideration. In the first place, warrants are freely traded over the counter or on one of the exchanges and so provide their owners with a fair measure of liquidity. Second, most warrants are exercisable for quite long periods of time, and in some cases they have infinite exercising periods. Third, the striking price of a warrant, unlike that of a call option, is not reduced by the value of any dividends. Finally, when the warrant is issued, the striking price often differs significantly from the price of the stock.

Because of this last characteristic, comparisons are facili-

176 / Convertible Securities

tated if both the price of the warrant and that of the stock are expressed as a percentage of the exercise price. It is then a simple matter to depict upper and lower limits within which the price of any warrant should lie. On the one hand, it can never fall below zero, nor can it fall below the price of the stock by much more than the exercise price, for such an event would offer an arbitrage profit to any investor who bought and exercised the warrant while shorting the stock. On the other hand, no investor would be justified in holding a warrant if it sold for more than the price of the stock itself, for the expected return from the warrant would then be inferior under every conceivable condition to the return from the stock. These upper and lower limits are illustrated by the 45° lines in Figure 34.

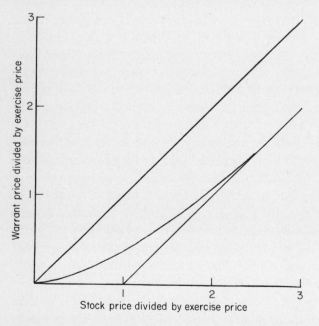

FIGURE 34. Expected relation between warrant price and stock price with maturity held constant (after Samuelson).[127]

The distance between these limits is usually far too wide to be of much practical guidance. The only time that Figure 34 defines the price of the warrant at all closely is when the stock price is well below the exercise price. In order to judge the value of the warrant under other conditions, it is necessary to make two assumptions. In the first place, it seems reasonable to suppose that investors who hold the common do so in the expectation that it will rise in price. Second, it is probable that investors only accept the additional risks of the warrant because they believe they will obtain a higher percentage return from their investment than they could expect from holding the stock. This will not be the case unless the warrant is likely to respond more sharply to a dollar rise in the stock price than to a dollar fall. In these circumstances, the relationship between the value of the two securities may be represented by a convex line such as the one shown in Figure 34.[127] When the stock price is sufficiently high, this convex line must intersect the lower limit of the warrant price. Beyond this point there is nothing to be gained by continuing to hold the warrant, and it will be exercised. If the stock price is subject to wide fluctuations, or if investors are satisfied with the expectation of only slightly higher returns from the warrant, the point of intersection will be relatively high; thus conversion will not take place until the stock price is well above the exercise price.

One problem with testing how closely warrants conform to this theory in practice is that it is difficult to separate changes in the price of a warrant that are due to changes in the price of the stock from those that may be due to the approach of the expiration date. This difficulty does not of course apply to perpetual warrants. Figure 35, therefore, compares the prices of the Alleghany Corporation perpetual warrant with those of the common stock during the period 1953–1964.[76] These points tend to lie along a convex line, which, if extended, would indicate that the warrant would be converted when the stock price was $4\frac{1}{2}$ times the exercise price. The degree of stock price volatility and the relative rates of return suggested by this curve coincide quite closely with the ones that occurred in practice.

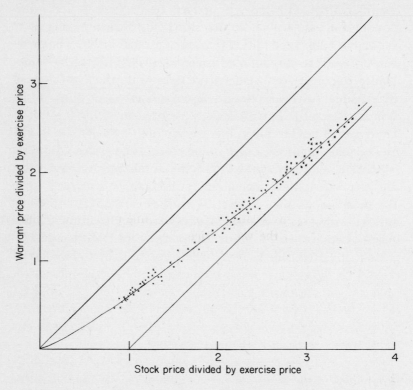

FIGURE 35. Relation between price of Alleghany Corporation perpetual warrant and price of Alleghany stock (after Kassouf).[76]

When one turns to dated warrants, the problem becomes more complex. Chapter 14 pointed out that the longer-dated options are more valuable simply because the price of the stock is likely to fluctuate more widely over the long term than over the short term. It was also suggested that since the variability of the share price increases roughly in proportion to the square root of the period under consideration, the value of the option should also vary with the square root of the time to maturity. For short-dated options this proved to be a good approximation. However, if carried to its logical limit, this notion would imply that an investor is justified in paying more for a very long dated option than for the stock itself. The problem arises from the fact that the limited liability of the stockholder restricts more and more the rate at which the spread of possible price movements can increase with time. It is because the stock cannot fall by more than 100% that it is never worth paying more for the warrant than for the stock.

The main point to bear in mind about the effect of duration is that at maturity the warrant must sell at its lower limit and that other things being equal, its value will increase with the duration of the warrant. Therefore, instead of drawing just one curve, as in Figure 34, it is necessary to draw a whole series of curves, each representing a different maturity date.[127] This is illustrated in Figure 36. Except in the special case of

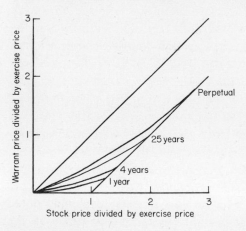

FIGURE 36. Expected relation between warrant price and stock price with varying maturities (after Samuelson).[127]

the perpetual warrant, the investor moves to progressively lower curves with the passage of time and to progressively higher points on each curve as the underlying stock appreciates. It is however only in the last years of a warrant's life that approaching maturity is likely to have a pronounced effect on the value of the warrant.

One other consideration needs to be introduced at this point. Since the owner of the warrant is not compensated for any dividend payments on the common stock, a warrant becomes less valuable when the common offers a high dividend yield.

There are many practical difficulties to assessing how closely warrant prices conform to this theory, but it is possible to verify its principal features by examining the variation in the prices of 43 warrants during the years 1945 to 1964.[77] In Figure 37 these prices have been plotted against those of the common stock. In contrast to the case of the Alleghany warrant, the values no longer cluster very closely along a single logarithmic curve. However, one can explain almost 90% of the variation in the warrant prices by fitting to the data an equation that takes into account both the level of the stock price and the term of the warrant. The manner in which the warrant prices appeared to respond to these two influences is shown in Figure 38. It confirms that other things being equal, the warrant price will decline with the approach of maturity, though the effect is pronounced only in the last year or two of the warrant's life. Given the term of the warrant, the relationship with the price of the stock can still be represented by a convex line, thus the warrant price comes to respond more sharply to changes in the stock price as the latter rises. The effect of the dividend yield is not easily distinguished from that of the stock price. Nevertheless, a somewhat better explanation of the variation in the warrant prices was secured by taking the yield differences into account as well.

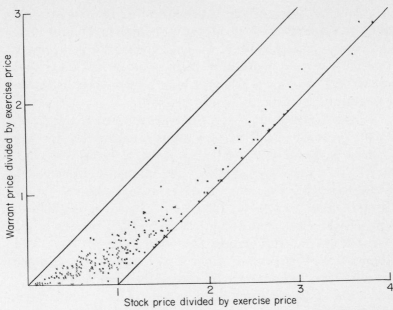

FIGURE 37. Relation between 234 warrant and stock prices (after Kassouf).[77]

In one major respect, this analysis fell short of a satisfactory test of the theory of warrant pricing. It was suggested earlier that other things being equal, the price of a warrant should be higher when the stock price is subject to wide fluctuations or when investors are satisfied with the expectation of only slightly higher returns from the warrant. The premium placed on longer-dated warrants provides some confirmation of the former suggestion, but there ought also to exist some connection between the price of the warrant and the volatility of the common stock. Similar studies, which have introduced a measure of volatility into the regression equation, have proved inconclusive.[136,137,151] This is in part because the estimates have been crude, but it is also because the variability of the stock price

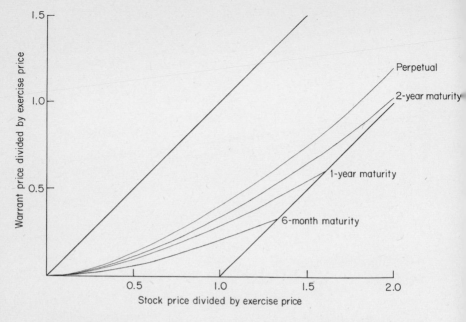

FIGURE 38. Relation between warrant price, stock price, and maturity, derived from regression of logs of 234 warrant prices on logs of stock prices and reciprocals of time to expiration (after Kassouf).[77]

has a twofold effect. On the one hand, it increases the expected return from the warrant; on the other, by increasing the riskiness of the warrant, it also induces investors to demand a higher return.

Before attempting to explore further the connection between the price of the warrant and the volatility of the stock, it may be useful to consider another exercise, which was concerned with the manner in which the price of the warrant is related to its duration, to the stock price, and to the dividend yield. The earlier discussion of the theory of warrant pricing pointed out that if investors require a higher return from the warrant than from the stock, some level of the stock price must exist

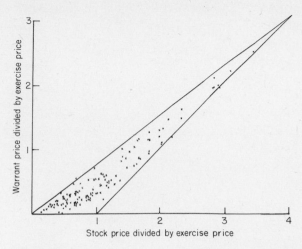

FIGURE 39. Relation between 157 warrant and stock prices. The enclosed area denotes the range of plausible relations (after Shelton).[136,137]

at which it will pay to exercise any warrant. An examination of the 157 warrant prices shown in Figure 39 indicates that in practice the premium has usually disappeared by the time the stock price has reached four times the exercise price. For this reason, Figure 39 defines some narrower limits within which most warrant prices can be expected to fall. The next step is to identify the factors that cause some of the warrants to sell close to the upper limit and others to sell near the lower limit. As one might expect from the earlier analysis, the price of a warrant appeared to be relatively low when it was near maturity or when the common offered a high dividend yield; in addition, the market seemed to place a lower value on unlisted warrants, presumably because they were by and large the riskier holdings. On the strength of these observations, the following rule of thumb was proposed.[136,137] To determine where within the zone of plausible prices a particular warrant should lie, the distance between the upper and lower limits should be multiplied by the formula

$$(0.47 - 4.25 \text{ yield} + 0.17 \text{ if the stock is listed})$$
$$\times \left[\frac{(\text{term in months})}{72} \right]^{1/4}.$$

In applying this formula, it was recommended that no warrant should be treated as if it had a maturity more distant than 120 months.

The warrant-stock relationships that are implied by such a rule are shown in Figure 40. The picture accords less well with

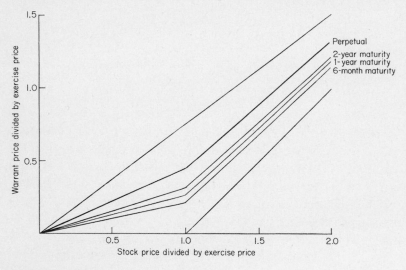

FIGURE 40. Relation between warrant price, stock price, and maturity, based on rule of thumb described in text, assuming warrant is listed and stock yields 2% (after Shelton).[136,137]

expectations than did Figure 38. In particular, it seems likely that short-dated warrants are converted somewhat earlier than this formula would indicate. Nevertheless, in most principal respects the relationships envisaged by this rule of thumb are reminiscent of those suggested by the more theoretical line of reasoning developed earlier.

This resemblance is really of interest only if it can also be shown that the warrant prices observed in practice are approximated quite closely by the rule of thumb. The first two columns of Table 38 suggest that this is the case. However, the corre-

TABLE 38. *Actual and Predicted Prices of 19 Warrants, November 1963*

	Actual Price	Predicted Price	Actual Premium	Predicted Premium
GenTire	49.50	51.46	0.03	0.10
Coast St Gas	23.75	24.21	0.04	0.08
Ala Gas	2.88	5.41	0.05	0.13
Textron	14.25	21.04	0.07	0.34
Hilton Hotel	3.50	7.35	0.08	0.16
Alleg Cp	6.63	7.09	0.10	0.22
McCrory	2.38	3.31	0.12	0.17
Armour	22.00	22.62	0.13	0.16
Telergstr	2.75	2.38	0.16	0.14
Trans W Air	12.50	17.52	0.18	0.44
Mack Tr 1971	8.63	7.75	0.19	0.17
Kerr Mc	16.75	17.45	0.21	0.22
Atlas Corp	1.38	1.70	0.22	0.27
Gen Accept	4.50	5.69	0.23	0.29
SymingtnW	7.00	5.91	0.24	0.17
MartinM	21.13	22.86	0.25	0.29
Mack Tr 1966	17.25	15.56	0.27	0.24
Pac Pet	5.88	4.75	0.31	0.25
SperryR	7.75	7.28	0.31	0.29

Source: After Shelton.[136,137]

spondence could be a misleading one, caused simply by differences in the absolute level of the stock price. A much more rigorous test would be to consider the predicted and actual premiums as a proportion of the exercise value. This is done in the final two columns of Table 38. Although on this basis the estimates are less impressive, there is still a significant degree of correlation between the two series.

Both the earlier regression analysis and this rougher exercise have cast some light on several of the principal factors that cause one warrant to be valued more highly than another. What they have not been able to distinguish is whether the market weighs these factors in a rational manner. A partial answer to this question can be had if it is assumed that warrants are exercisable only at the end of a specific period. Figure 32 demonstrates that over such a period the distribution of possible returns from a warrant is directly linked to the distribution of possible changes in the price of the stock. When the latter distribution is normal, the expected value of the warrant can be defined in terms of the exercise price, the current stock price, the expected change in the stock price, and the spread of possible changes in the stock price. If estimates could be obtained of these last two quantities, it would be possible to compute the expected value of the warrant and compare it to the price.

One might begin by assuming that the market expects the stock price to remain unchanged. The problem then is to estimate the dispersion of possible stock price changes. This is complicated by the fact that the dispersion depends on the length of time that investors expect to hold the warrant. While in the case of puts and calls it was reasonable to assume that the market's horizon generally coincides with the length of the option, this is unlikely to be the case with long-dated warrants. One solution is to select a plausible value for the dispersion of possible stock price changes and on the basis of this conjecture calculate the expected value of the warrant over a number of successive weeks. These expected values can then be compared to the actual market prices of the warrant. This exercise can be repeated with different estimates of the dispersion until it is no longer possible to obtain a set of expected values that correspond more closely to the prices of the warrant. If the correlation between the two series proved to be consistently weak, there would be some justification for doubting whether the warrant price properly reflected the market's assessment of the stock. Thirty series of warrant prices were therefore chosen for analysis in this way.[141] With very few exceptions, there existed a figure for the variation of possible stock price changes that implied a set of expected warrant values, closely related to the actual warrant prices. To check that this is not simply a coincidence, it is worth examining the 30 estimates of the anticipated spread of price changes. Although some part of the variation in these estimates is likely to stem from the fact that the market's horizon may differ from one warrant to another, it should also to some degree reflect differences in the amount of annual fluctuation in the price of each stock. This proves to be the case. This involved but original approach to the subject has confirmed that differences in warrant prices result largely from a rational assessment of each warrant's expected value and that in making this assessment the market is strongly influenced by the volatility of the stock.

Much less is known about the average experience of the warrant holder than about that of the option trader. Table 39 shows the average annual return between 1956 and 1962 of the warrants cited in Standard & Poor's Stock Guide, together with the rates of return both from the associated stock and from a market index.[136,137] The behavior of the stocks was very closely dependent on that of the market, though they were subject to wider price fluctuations. While the shareholder could have offset these additional risks by investing a proportion of his money in short-term government bonds, his overall return would have fallen $1\frac{1}{2}\%$ short of the market return. These observations apply even more strongly to the warrants. Their behavior was also heavily dependent on that of the market, but in this case an extra 1% change in the index led

TABLE 39. *Realized Rates of Return from Warrants*

	Change in Price of Warrants	Approximate Return from Associated Stocks	Return from Standard & Poor's Composite Index
Dec. 1956–Dec. 1957	−35%	−28%	−10%
Dec. 1957–Dec. 1958	+62	+54	+41
Dec. 1958–Dec. 1959	+26	+19	+12
Dec. 1959–Nov. 1960	−26	+ 1	− 4
Nov. 1960–Dec. 1961	+60	+25	+32
Dec. 1961–Dec. 1962	−33	−16	− 9
Average Annual Return	9.0%	9.3%	10.2%

Source: After Shelton.[136,137]

to an extra 2.1% change in the price of the warrant. Again an investor could have exactly offset this additional leverage by holding a combination of warrants and bonds, but in these circumstances his return would have been 2% less than that on the index. In sum, the performance of the warrants was worse than that of the underlying stocks and markedly worse than that of the general equity market.

Dramatic support for this view was provided by an analysis of the effect of taking successive short positions between 1946 and 1966 in a selection of warrants with less than four years to expiration.[149] Despite the fact that the underlying stocks rose by an average of 18%, the value of the 11 warrants declined by 88%. In judging these results, it is essential to bear in mind that the precise criteria used to select these warrants were devised with the advantage of hindsight. Nevertheless, there seems good reason to believe that short-dated warrants offer little compensation for the very high risks involved.

There is a widespread belief that the issue of warrants automatically benefits the company concerned. One commentator has argued that by issuing a warrant with a high exercise price the company may be able to raise deferred equity at a desirable price. If this does not prove to be the case and the warrants are not exercised, the proceeds of the sale remain as a clear profit to the company.[75] The suspicious element in this notion is that it is inconsistent with the position of the option writer. When an investor sells a call, he profits to the extent of the premium if the call is not exercised. If the call is taken up, he must offset against this premium the difference between the exercise price and the actual stock price on the exercise date. A company that sells a warrant is in an identical position. If the warrant is never exercised, the company profits from the proceeds of the sale. If it is exercised, the company must offset against these proceeds the opportunity cost of selling stock at the exercise price instead of at the actual price on the exercise date.

Jack Spratt's Law is basic in finance. If two parties have different tastes, they may be able to reach an agreement that benefits both. In the absence of any such differences, no purely financial arrangement can benefit one group except at the expense of another. There are some indications that the experience of the warrant holder has been unsatisfactory except for investors with unusual tastes or opportunities. In other words, the company seems to be able to shift a larger proportion of its risks than of its opportunities to the warrant holder. It is here that the principal justification for warrant financing lies.

Chapter 17 Convertible Debentures

Consider the following hypothetical situation. Shares X, Y, and Z are all quoted at $80 and offer a dividend yield that is equal to the rate of interest on corporate bonds. The three firms have a declared policy of leaving their dividends unchanged. Where the companies differ is in their approach to raising new capital. Company X decides to sell a twenty-year debenture, which is convertible for a period of five years on the basis of one share of common for each $100 nominal value. The issue is placed at par, which fairly reflects the value that it would have in the absence of any convertible feature. Company Y adopts a different policy. It sells at par a twenty-year bond, attached to which is a five-year warrant to buy one share at $100. The third company, Z, also offers a package, but in this case for each $100 the investor receives one share of common stock together with a five-year option to sell it back to the company for $100.

Except for divergences in the way these issues are treated by the Internal Revenue, the three schemes differ only in detail. In every instance the investor will come to own the common stock if by the end of five years its price has risen by a minimum of 25%. If this does not occur, he will either possess a corporate bond or will obtain cash that can then be invested in such a bond. Hence, a convertible debenture can be viewed as an issue of debt with a warrant attached or as an issue of stock with a put option attached.

As in the case of warrants or options, one can define limits within which the price of the convertible must fall. These are illustrated in Figure 41. Arbitrage opportunities will prevent the convertible from persistently selling below its value as a bond or as a stock, and few investors could be persuaded to

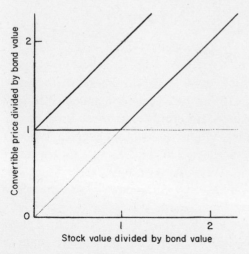

FIGURE 41. Limits on price of convertible debenture relative to value as a bond and as a stock.

hold a convertible that was worth more than the bond and the equivalent amount of stock put together. The difference between these limits and the bond value is identical to the limits on the value of a warrant. By the same token, the distance between these limits and the stock value corresponds to the possible range of prices that can rationally be paid for a put.

At this stage, it is merely necessary to note that the location of the price of the debenture within these limits recalls in a general way the relationship between the prices of the warrant and the stock. As a demonstration of this, Figure 42 depicts the prices of 199 convertible debentures in February 1970. The difference between the debenture price and its minimum value appears to be greatest when the common stands at the

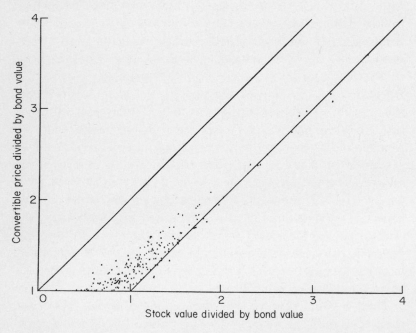

FIGURE 42. Relation between prices of 199 convertible debentures and stocks.

implied exercise price and becomes progressively less marked as the price of the common departs from this level. However, compared with the similar diagrams of warrant prices, the points in Figure 42 seem to lie rather closer to the lower limit. If this parallel is a fair one, it suggests that the market places a lower value on a warrant attached to a bond than it places on warrants that are not so encumbered.

Some commentators have argued that no part even of this modest premium on the convertible debenture arises from the option feature.[154] The view is a disturbing one, for it implies that options have no particular value as a hedging device. The justification of this view rests on the belief that the advantages of the conversion feature can be obtained by other means at little cost. Consider, for example, the case of a convertible selling at its stock value, which in turn is 10% ahead of its bond value. If the price of the common rises, the convertible must rise in the same proportion. On the other hand, as long as the debt is secure, the convertible can fall by only 10%, whereas there is no limit to the amount by which the stock can fall. Yet this is not the only way in which an investor can protect himself against a decline in the price of the common. A simple alternative is to buy the stock and simultaneously place a stop order to sell it at a price 10% below its current level and reinvest the proceeds in a bond. If this order were ever executed, the investor would need to place a stop order to buy back the stock on any rise in price and sell the bond. Thus, by always leaving an order to buy or sell the stock at the appropriate price, the investor should be able to participate fully in any price movement above that level and yet protect himself against any decline below it.

There is something far too good to be true about this argument. Certainly the stockholders must have thought that they were parting with something of value when the bond was made convertible, for the effect is to leverage the company if things go badly and diffuse the ownership if they go well. Moreover, whereas investment in common stock has hitherto appeared a very risky occupation, it now seems that these risks can be contained without any diminution of the potential gains. If it were true that this alternative strategy gave the investor all the protection of the convertible debenture at far less cost, then the only justification for a premium on the convertible would be such incidental advantages as the higher current income. The fallacy lies in the suggestion that the costs of such a policy are trivial. Even if one ignores the fact that stop orders are frequently not executed at the trigger price, the investor becomes liable for the transaction costs of selling the stock. If the price moves back and forth past the trigger price, the costs of repeatedly buying and selling the stock at the same level may cumulate rapidly. The owner of the convertible debenture at least knows how much he has paid to insure against a fall in the price of the common, but the investor who relies on a series of stop orders has no guarantee as to the ultimate size of his insurance premium. This is a strange kind of insurance.

The belief that the convertible premium differs in character from an option premium is not based solely on theoretical reasoning. Some support for the view was provided by an analysis of the prices of a large sample of convertible debentures whose stock value exceeded their bond value.[154] It was hypothesized that if investors do value the protection afforded by the implied put option, the premium on these bonds must be inversely related to the maximum loss that the holder can suffer, namely, the difference between the price of the convertible and its value as a bond. If investors are not willing to pay for this feature, the premium can be due only to such incidental advantages as the higher income on the convertible and the lower brokerage charges. Multiple regression was therefore used to estimate the manner in which the premium varied with the increased income, the saving in commission expenses, and the potential loss. Whereas the first two factors appeared to explain a large part of the difference in the premium, there was no indication that the market placed any more value on convertibles that afforded good protection against the effect of a fall in the price of the common.

The analysis is ingenious but the conclusion suspect. In the first place, the smaller the transaction cost advantage to the bond, the larger appeared to be the premium accorded to it. It is difficult to believe that investors welcome an excuse to pay larger brokerage commissions. The explanation seems to be that the transaction cost advantage is least when the stock value is closest to the bond value, so that the relationship between transaction costs and premium may simply reflect the fact that the premium disappears as the stock price rises. Similar doubts center on the effect of the income differential, for this also varies with the stock value. Such a connection between the premium and the stock value may have nothing to do with the differences in income or brokerage costs, for it could stem from recognition of the fact that the put option offers less protection against a fall in the price of the common when the latter is in excess of the conversion price. It may in this case seem odd that the analysis did not uncover any worthwhile relationship between the size of the premium and the potential loss. However, by defining the potential loss to include the premium, any strong inverse connection between the two was scarcely possible.

If convertibles are regarded by investors as a mixture of a security and an option, one would expect to find that convertible prices respond to the same influences that affect the price of a warrant or an option. Some general assurance that this is the case was provided by an analysis of 164 convertible debentures floated between 1948 and 1963.[114,115] Almost half of the variation in the price of the implied call option could be explained in terms of three factors: the level of the stock price relative to the conversion price, the appreciation that investors appeared to look for in the stock, and the degree to which the stock price fluctuated. The price of this option also appeared to be inversely related to the dividend yield on the common.

In order to understand something of the manner in which the market weighs these factors, it is once again useful to assume that the option can be exercised only on one specific date. Figure 32 in Chapter 14 may serve as a reminder that the expected return from the option is then determined by the exercise price and the possible changes in the price of the stock by the exercise date.

One investigation along these lines sought to measure the extent to which the price of a convertible approximated the stock value plus the expected gain from a two-year put option.[11] The last quantity was calculated on the assumption that investors regarded former rates of gain from the stock as liable to recur with the same frequency. The first column of Table 40 shows the price of 7 convertibles estimated in this way, and the second column shows the actual price. Although there is a pronounced tendency for the estimates to

TABLE 40. *Actual and Estimated Prices of 7 Convertible Debentures, June 1962*

Issue	Estimated Price	Actual Price
Homestke	161	137
Northrop	150	120
Burrghs	102	115
SCM Cp	94	108
Rohr Cp	104	106
AllegLud	91	99
FoodFair	92	99

Source: After Baumol, Malkiel, and Quandt.[11]

exaggerate the differences in the bond prices, they are very successful at ranking the issues in order of price. Unfortunately, this achievement is less impressive than may at first appear, for one could probably have done nearly as well on this test by assuming that the convertible simply rested on its lower limit. In judging these results, it is important to bear in mind that the method employed to value the option was very rough and ready. One cannot assume that the market believes there is a 50% chance that the stock will appreciate at a 10% annual rate just because the price has risen by 10% in five of the last ten years. Furthermore, each option was valued as if it were exercisable only at the end of two years, and no attempt was made to discount the expected gains. It is reasonable to suppose that if these deficiencies could have been made good, the estimated prices would have been much closer to the actual ones.

A more elaborate analysis was made of the sample of 164 debentures.[114,115] Each was regarded as a combination of a bond and a call option on the stock, but instead of simply assuming that the option could be exercised only at the end of two years, the exercise date was taken to be the one that would maximize the value of the option. It was pointed out in Chapter 14 that if the price changes of the stock are distributed normally, it is necessary to know only the expected change in the price of the stock and the dispersion of the possible changes in order to be able to compute the expected profit from the option. For want of any better alternative, it was assumed that the market expected each stock to appreciate at the same rate as in earlier years and to remain equally variable. On this basis, 80% of the variation in the implied option price could be explained in terms of the expected profit from the option.

It is likely that in valuing the conversion privilege the market also allows for the fact that the variety of possible outcomes is much higher in the case of some options than of others. Not surprisingly, therefore, an even better explanation of differences in the implied option price could be secured by taking into account both the expected profit and the spread of possible consequences. One other consideration appeared to affect the price. Just as in the case of puts and calls, the market seemed to prefer convertibles that offered a combination of a small chance of a very large profit and a large chance of a very small loss to those that offered a more balanced set of odds.

These results constitute strong confirmation that the market does look upon convertibles as a combination of a security and an option and that the variation in the price of the option reflects a rational appraisal of the opportunities and risks involved. However, before looking more closely at the implications, it is worth reviewing some of the assumptions involved. Throughout this chapter it has been assumed that the underlying bond value of the debenture remains constant. In practice, not only will it vary but the movement is likely to be in part related to changes in the stock price, for any news that lowers the value of the stock will also cast doubt on the security of the bond. To the extent that the bond and the stock move in parallel, the value of an option to convert from one to another is decreased. This is an important consideration for convertibles issued by small and unseasoned companies.

It is worth digressing for a moment to note that the limitations of the one-period assumption can be reduced at the sacrifice of realism in other respects. This is done by subdividing the life of the option into a number of short periods. Since the option becomes worthless when it matures, its value one interval before expiration must depend solely on the possible changes in the price of the stock over the remaining portion of its life. One period earlier still, the value of the option will be equal to that of a short-term option plus the value that it possesses at the end of this time. Therefore, given some measure of the possible stock price movements during these intervals, it should be possible to work back from the value of the option at expiration to its value at any other time. One study sought to explain in this way the prices of 40 convertible debentures at the end of March 1962.[44] The prospective changes in the stock price were estimated from an analysis of the way in which the stock had responded in the past to variations in the market level, and the risks associated with the convertible were assumed to lie partway between those of a simple bond and those of the stock itself, the proportions being fixed by the relation between the debenture's stock value and its bond value. This information was used to derive estimates of the value of the debenture at the end of each year, assuming that the investor intended to hold it for at least another year. Finally, some allowance was made for the possibility that the company would force conversion or that higher dividend payments on the common would make conversion advisable. In Table 41, the estimated value of each debenture is compared with the actual price. Once again the option analogy seems to be appropriate, since 89% of the variation in the premium over the stock value could be explained in terms of the estimated value of the implicit put option.

Attention has already been drawn to the fact that the price of the convertible generally lies closer to its lower limit than the price of a warrant, and Table 41 provides some further indication that convertibles are not seriously overvalued. For a more detailed assessment of the returns expected from the implied call options it is necessary to return to the analysis of 164 debentures.[114,115] It was estimated that on the average the market anticipated an annual return of 11.7% from the 164 stocks. Since the rate of interest during this period was about 4%, the holder appeared to require an additional 7.7% to compensate for the risks that he incurred. The annual rate of return expected from the conversion option was 53%. If allowance is again made for the fact that it was possible to obtain 4% from

TABLE 41. *Actual and Estimated Prices of 40 Convertible Debentures, March 1962*

Issue	Actual Price	Estimated Price	Stock Value
Case JI	69	77	32
Douglas Air	81	82	32
Vanadium	91	89	44
DressInd	102	89	54
Flintkote	104	91	52
FoodFair	108	112	94
PanAm WAir	108	101	75
CopwlStl	108	102	75
McCall	109	111	87
Eastrn St	110	107	71
CombEn	110	107	97
AlliedStr	110	101	88
AllegLud	110	103	83
Nat Cyl Gas	111	98	58
AutoCan	111	102	68
Gen Tim	112	110	69
Brunswk	113	101	67
Fansteel Inc	114	107	77
City Prod	115	110	98
ChampP	116	100	76
Armour	116	114	92
GrandUn	117	115	98
Am Distill	117	117	103
Boeing Co	119	116	100
UnAirLin	121	119	98
HookerC	123	109	80
Rohr Cp	123	122	115
Nat AirLin	127	133	107
Int Silver	134	133	124
SCM Cp	135	132	114
Aldens	136	142	134
Spiegel	136	133	122
Burrghs	137	134	126
Northrop	139	140	134
Balt GE	152	153	153
US Fregt	153	149	149
InterstStr	163	164	163
Lockheed Air	207	202	202
Macy RH	212	207	207
Avco Cp	238	235	235

Source: After Duvel.[44]

a riskless bond, the purchaser of convertible bonds appears to have needed an additional return of 49% from the amount that he paid over bond value. This is a large reward indeed, more than six times that required by the common stockholder. However, this part of the convertible bondholder's investment is a very risky venture. Although the portion of his funds represented by the bond value of the convertible is well protected against loss, the money invested in the option is much less secure, for unless the common comes to exceed the exercise price, the option is worthless. It is not therefore surprising to find that on average the option appeared to be nearly six times as risky as the common stock. This result is very important, for if the additional return on the option is almost exactly balanced by the increased risk, an investor could neither have increased nor reduced his expected return for a given degree of risk by holding convertible bonds instead of a combination of ordinary bonds and common stocks.

Usually, when one looks at securities that offer the expectation of very high rates of return, one finds that the risks involved are even more extreme. This appears to be true of the most volatile stocks[116] and of options and warrants. Speculators whose dreams of wealth exceed their access to borrowed funds have no alternative but to compete to acquire such securities, even if the additional prospective returns are not commensurate with the increased risks. It is interesting, therefore, that the options associated with convertible bonds do not appear to be unusually expensive. One reason for this is that the option is not detachable; thus, in order to acquire an option worth about $100, an investor is obliged to take up a bond costing ten times that sum. Before the imposition of margin requirements, the investor could effectively detach a large part of the bond by borrowing against it. However, the difference between his borrowing cost and the interest rate on the bond could increase the cost of the option sharply. If it is true that the

202 / Convertible Securities

price of the conversion option would be raised considerably by being made detachable, one is left wondering why the issuing companies do not prefer to sell bonds with detachable warrants.

So far the discussion has been concerned with the rates of return that the market appeared to expect. The conclusions are highly dependent on the assumption that the market expected former rates of return on the stock to be repeated. In the case of the common stocks, the realized returns proved to be much less than this. Indeed, over the four-year period following the issue of the debentures the stocks declined slightly in price. This may have been a coincidence, or it may indicate a tendency for managements to issue convertibles when they suspect that their stocks are overvalued.

Many of the stocks performed quite differently from the average, so that while a number of the conversion options became almost worthless, others provided exceptionally high rates of return. These extremes were so great in the case of the lower-priced options as to make the calculation of a single average rate of return distinctly misleading. Nevertheless, it is clear that in general the conversion option proved not only very risky but also very profitable. The average cost of this option was $13 per $100 bond. Yet within four years nearly a quarter of the bonds had been called at a premium of $50 over bond value, and the remainder could have been sold in the market at an average premium of $28 over bond value.

Nothing has been adduced in this chapter to disturb or delight the convertible holder, for typically his investment appears to offer fair compensation for the risks involved. Unless the investor is strongly attracted by the lottery characteristics of the convertible, there is little to choose between purchase of a convertible security or a package of debts and equity.

Several surveys of corporate motives for the sale of convertibles have indicated that the majority of the issuing companies regard their action as a means of raising deferred equity capital at an attractive price and that a somewhat smaller proportion look on it as a way of selling low-yielding debt.[25,104,113] To consider convertible debentures in either light is not helpful. They are not low-coupon debt: they are a combination of an appropriately priced corporate bond and an option. The deferred equity view is applicable only if management is confident that the option will be exercised. In these circumstances, the issue of a convertible benefits existing shareholders more than a simple issue of common stock but is less desirable than the sale of debt. Indeed, the general principles of option writing suggest that the sale of convertibles will prove to be only the optimal strategy if the price of the common does not change substantially from its level at the time of issue.

One study of convertible financing has detected a slight tendency for the market to place more value on the profits of companies whose bonds are convertible, but the effect was too weak to be meaningful.[21] More generally, the empirical evidence in this chapter has suggested that in practice the sale of convertible debentures provides neither cheap debt nor cheap equity but something akin to a fairly priced mixture of the two.

CONCLUSION

Efficient Capital Markets
and Financial Policy

There are in the United States almost 20,000 professional security analysts and almost 30 million shareholders. Many of these may be inactive, and others may be foolish, but there also undoubtedly exists a substantial number who are both energetic and well informed. Given such competition, it would be surprising if important, publicly available information tended to go unnoticed for long.

It is no less likely that the majority of these investors have certain objectives in common. First and foremost, their concern lies in the profit that they might earn from their investment. The name of the company, its business, the color of the stock certificate, or the refreshments at the stockholders' meeting are all incidental considerations. However, the identity of interest usually goes well beyond this simple fact, for most investors appear to regard more wealth as preferable to less and to regard certain wealth as preferable to uncertain. There are those who enjoy gambling even in the face of a probable loss, but the vast majority of invested funds belong to individuals who are to some degree averse to risk.

It is this picture of a large number of investors competing to achieve substantially similar ends that has prompted the suggestion that for the majority of the participants investment is a fair game.[46] Public information comes to be so rapidly impounded in the price of a stock that a purchaser can expect neither more nor less than a fair reward for the risks involved. My earlier volume discussed some empirical tests of this notion, dwelling principally on the strong relationship between the risks and rewards of investment in common stocks. The present work has been concerned with a much greater diversity of topics. Some of these are important in their own right; others are of no more than peripheral interest. Yet taken together this seeming medley constitutes valuable evidence in favor of the fair game analogy.

There were a number of indications that investors are occupied only with events that affect the substantive value of the enterprise. Changes in the company's distribution policy or in its financial structure were shown to affect the stock price only insofar as they altered the after-tax return on capital. The market's efficiency was revealed in its ability to appreciate the significance of any item of news. The principal evidence here was found in the discussion of stock splits and secondary distributions. In both cases, the market appeared to make a remarkably correct assessment of the odds that some more momentous company news was in the offing. Finally, the speed of the market's adjustment proved to be no less impressive than its accuracy. Numerous instances were observed of its swift response to information. It was apparent in the way prices adjusted to the announcement of earnings or dividends, to the publication of economic news, or to explicit or implicit statements of professional opinion.

It is a human tendency to make a divine law from empirical observations, but in fact the fair game theory should not be accepted without some qualification. In the first place, there appear to be circumstances in which investors, either out of ignorance or out of a love of gambling, persistently accept unfavorable odds. Such is the case for option traders and for short sellers. The market's reaction to new information has not always been unbiased. There seems, for example, to have been a slight tendency for investors to be misled by the publicity that accompanies new issues or new listings. A more striking case was suggested by the analysis of insider trading. Presumably because of the lack of publicity given to the *Official Summary,* the implications of its contents appear to have been almost wholly ignored. Finally, it is important to bear in mind that although prices have adjusted swiftly to new information, the effect has not been instantaneous. In each case, the bulk of the adjustment occurred on the day of the announcement, but the remainder of the process was typically spread over about a week.

These examples do not necessarily imply any lack of efficiency. Dealing costs may limit the extent to which traders can profit from delays in the adjustment of prices to new information, and no matter how alert the bulk of the participants may be, there is no way that they can profit from the knowledge that by most standards the option market is not a fair game. But whatever the interpretation placed on these cases, it does not affect the broad picture of a competitive marketplace in which security prices reflect all the available relevant information. This constitutes important indirect evidence for the suggestion that security prices follow approximately a random walk, for in such a market prices will respond only to news that could not be inferred from earlier events.

If the fair game analogy is appropriate, the investor must face the fact that while he can fairly easily match the performance of the average stockholder, considerable skill is needed to do any better than this. Some have gone so far as to argue that the difficulty of gaining superior information is such that unless an investor possesses the particular advantage of the insider or the specialist, he cannot expect to achieve superior performance with any consistency. It is true that studies of the performance of professionally managed funds have failed to reveal any widespread superiority,[70] but no evidence has been adduced as to how far the experience of individual managers departs from that of the group. There is little likelihood that these distinctions are important, but it is taking a naïvely simple view of the world to believe that the differences in forecasting ability that were observed in Chapter 7 are never translated into differences in portfolio performance.

For this reason, it is worth considering some of the preconditions for investment success. If an institution is going to secure superior results, it will not be with the sole aid of public information, whether that information be the earnings record, management's most recent statement, or a brokerage firm's most recent circular. Hence, it is not enough to employ average analysts to do average things. It is far better to purchase for the same sum a smaller number of analysts whose unusual familiarity with the industry and capacity for hard work can lead to an understanding of the situation that is not always possessed by everybody else. If such analysts are to be effective, it is important that the organizational structure should be such as to encourage them to concentrate their attention on areas where they have a comparative advantage and to produce recommendations only when they have good reason to feel the prospective rate of return is abnormally high or low.

Neither condition is likely to be met if each analyst is compelled to comment at frequent intervals on a large number of securities. External advice can contribute little toward superior performance unless others are ignorant of its existence or its worth, but the rarity of useful advice suggests that it should be drawn from a wide variety of sources. Finally, a fund manager is likely to make the best use of resources only if he receives a systematic appraisal of his own performance and that of his advisors.

Such then are the primary conditions for superior investment performance. Yet it is important to bear in mind that if the fair game theory is correct, the fund rate of return is likely to depend far more on the amount of risk that is incurred than on any secret knowledge on the part of the fund's manager. In these circumstances, the crucial task for any institution is to assess the maximum degree of risk that can prudently be tolerated and then to select a portfolio that accords with this decision. The difficulty of these tasks is not less than their importance.

Much of this book has been concerned with the effect of corporate financial policy on the price of the stock. Retained earnings, issues of common stock, debt, convertible debt, and warrants were all touched upon. The overriding impression to emerge is that the market is indifferent to the financial structure, except insofar as it results in an increase in the after-tax return on invested capital. The tax subsidy on the use of debt has just this effect, and the value of the equity consequently rises by roughly the value of the subsidy. However, the much smaller tax advantage to retained earnings seems to go largely unrecognized; thus retentions do not provide cheaper capital than other sources. There is one other circumstance that could affect the market's attitude to a company's financial structure. Speculators with ambitions of great wealth frequently have little alternative but to bid up the price of high-risk securities as long as they continue to offer some improvement in prospective returns. By issuing warrants, a company may be able to reduce the risk of the common stock without a corresponding diminution in the expected return.

The chapters on corporate financial policy also serve as a useful reminder of the avidity with which the market scrutinizes a company's actions. Changes in the payout ratio, the announcement of a stock split, the application for an Exchange quotation — all matters that are of little importance in themselves — take on significance just because they are usually associated with changes in company prosperity. This places a responsibility on management to avoid actions that are liable to misinterpretation.

Finally, there are some major economic implications to these findings. The broad arguments for a competitive environment are no less applicable to the securities markets than to manufacturing industry. Mankind is not endowed with perfect foresight, so it is foolish to complain that capital is often misdirected. One can, however, reasonably judge the efficiency of the securities markets by the extent to which each company's cost of capital is determined by a rational and unbiased assessment of all available relevant information. The extensive general testimony on this question was buttressed by more specific evidence that companies can raise new funds at the going market rate. Rights issues and new unseasoned issues can both be made without offering the inducement of abnormally high rates of return.

Company Names and Abbreviations

The following is a listing of companies referred to in this book, together with the abbreviations used for them in tables and figures.

Company	*Abbreviation*
Acme Steel Company	Acme St
Alabama Gas Corporation	Ala Gas
Aldens, Incorporated	Aldens
Alleghany Corporation	Alleg Cp
Allegheny Ludlum Steel Corporation	AllegLud
Allied Stores Corporation	AlliedStr
Allis-Chalmers Manufacturing Company	Allis Chalm
Aluminum Company of America	Alcoa

Company	*Abbreviation*
American Agricultural Chemical Company	Am Ag Chem
American Airlines, Incorporated	Am Airlin
American Distilling Company	Am Distill
American Investment Company	AmInvest
American News Company	Am News
American Precision Industries, Inc.	Am Precisn
The American Tobacco Company	Am Tob
American Water Works Co., Inc.	Am WatWks
Armour & Company	Armour
Associated Dry Goods Corporation	Assd DG
Atlas Corporation	Atlas Corp
Automatic Canteen Company of America	AutoCan
Avco Corporation	Avco Cp
Avon Products Incorporated	AvonPd
Baltimore Gas & Electric Company	Balt GE
Beech-Nut Life Savers, Inc.	Beech-Nut
Boeing Company	Boeing Co
Brunswick Corporation	Brunswk
Burroughs Corporation	Burrghs
Carter Products, Inc.	CarterPd
Case (J. I.) Company	Case JI
Caterpillar Tractor Company	CaterTr
Champion Papers, Incorporated	ChampP
City Products Corporation	City Prod
Coastal States Gas Producing Company	Coast St Gas
Combustion Engineering, Inc.	CombEn
Commercial Credit Company	Com Credit
Control Data Corporation	Control Data
Copperweld Steel Company	CopwlStl
Detroit Steel Corporation	Det Steel
Distillers Corporation–Seagrams, Ltd.	DistSeag
Douglas Aircraft Company	Douglas Air
Dover Corporation	Dover Cp
Dresser Industries, Incorporated	DressInd

Company	*Abbreviation*
Eastern Stainless Steel Corp.	Eastrn St
Echo Incorporated	Echo
Fansteel, Incorporated	Fansteel Inc
Federal Mogul Corporation	FedMog
Flintkote Company	Flintkote
Food Fair Stores, Incorporated	FoodFair
General Acceptance Corporation	Gen Accept
General American Oil Company of Texas	GAmOil
General Cable Corporation	GnCable
General Dynamics Corporation	GenDynam
General Electric Company	Gen Elec
General Time Corporation	Gen Tim
General Tire & Rubber Company	GenTire
Georgia-Pacific Corporation	Ga Pac
Grand Union Company	GrandUn
Granite City Steel Company	GraniteC
Grant (W. T.) Company	GrantW
Great Atlantic & Pacific Tea Company, Inc.	Gt A & P
Heller (Walter E.) & Company	Heller
Hilton Hotels Corporation	Hilton Hotel
Homestake Mining Company	Homestke
Hooker Chemical Corporation	HookerC
Hormel (Geo. A.) & Company	Hormel GA
Ideal Cement Company	Ideal Cem
International Silver Company	Int Silver
International Telephone & Telegraph Corporation	IntT&T
Interstate Department Stores, Inc.	InterstStr
Kerr-McGee Oil Industries, Incorporated	Kerr Mc
Kimberly-Clark Corporation	KimbClk
Lehigh Portland Cement Company	LehPCem
Libby, McNeill & Libby	Libb McN
Lockheed Aircraft Corporation	Lockheed Air

Company	Abbreviation
Mack Trucks, Incorporated	Mack Tr
Macy (R. H.) & Company, Inc.	Macy RH
Marshall Field & Company	MarshFD
Martin Marietta Corporation	MartinM
McCall Corporation	McCall
McCrory Corporation	McCrory
McLouth Steel Corporation	McLouth
Merck & Company, Inc.	Merck
Minnesota Enterprises Incorporated	MinnEntrp
Mohasco Industries, Incorporated	Mohasco
Morrell (John) & Company	J Morrell
National Airlines Incorporated	Nat Airlin
National Cylinder Gas Company	Nat Cyl Gas
National Distillers & Chemical Corporation	Nat Distil
National Gypsum Company	NatGyps
National Tea Company	Nat Tea
Northrop Corporation	Northrop
Pacific Petroleums Ltd.	Pac Pet
Pan-American World Airways, Inc.	PanAm WAir
Parke, Davis & Company	ParkeDav
Philip Morris Incorporated	PhilMorr
Phillips Petroleum Company	Phill Pet
Pure Oil Company	Pure Oil
Revlon, Incorporated	Revlon
Richfield Oil Corporation	Richfd Oil
Rohr Corporation	Rohr Cp
San Diego Gas & Electric Company	SDiegoG
SCM Corporation	SCM Cp
Seaboard World Airlines, Inc.	Sbd World Air
Sears, Roebuck & Company	Sears Ro
Sperry Rand Corporation	SperryR
Spiegel, Incorporated	Spiegel
Starrett (L. S.) Company	Starrett
Stokely–Van Camp, Incorporated	StokeVC

Company	Abbreviation
Sun Oil Company	Sun Oil
Sunray DX Oil Company	Sunray Oil
Sunshine Biscuits Inc.	SunshBis
Symington Wayne Corporation	SymingtnW
Talcott (James), Incorporated	Talcott
Tasminex N. L.	Tasminex
Teleregister Corporation	Telergstr
Textron Inc.	Textron
Timken Roller Bearing Co.	Timken
Trans World Airlines, Inc.	Trans W Air
Twentieth Century–Fox Film Corporation	Twen Cent
United Air Lines, Incorporated	UnAirLin
United Biscuit Company of America	Un Bis
United States Freight Company	US Fregt
United States Gypsum Company	USGypsm
United States Steel Corporation	US Steel
Universal American Corporation	UnivAm
Vanadium Corporation of America	Vanadium
Van Raalte Company, Inc.	Van Raalte
Virginia Chemicals Inc.	Va Chemcl
White Motor Corporation	WhteMot
Wrigley (Wm., Jr.) Company	Wrigley
Wyandotte Industries	Wyand Ind
Xerox Corporation	Xerox Cp

References

1. Adams, D. F. "The Effect on Stock Price from Listing on the New York Stock Exchange." M.B.A. thesis, New York University, 1965.

2. Allen, F. B. "Does Going into Debt Lower the 'Cost of Capital'?" *Financial Analysts Journal* 10 (August 1954): 57–61.

3. Arditti, F. D. "Risk and the Required Return on Equity."*Journal of Finance* 22 (March 1967): 19–36.

4. Ashley, J. W. "Stock Prices and Changes in Earnings and Dividends: Some Empirical Results." *Journal of Political Economy* 70 (February 1962): 82–85.

5. Atkinson, T. R. *The Pattern of Financial Asset Ownership*. Princeton, N.J.: Princeton University Press, 1956.

6. Bachelier, L. "Théorie de la Spéculation." Docteur ès Sciences Mathématiques dissertation, University of Paris, 1900. Translated

into English by A. J. Boness as "Theory of Speculation," in *The Random Character of Stock Market Prices,* edited by P. H. Cootner (Cambridge, Mass.: M.I.T. Press, 1964), pp. 17–78.

7. Bailey, M. "Capital Gains and Income Taxation." Unpublished paper.

8. Bank Administration Institute. *Measuring the Investment Performance of Pension Funds.* Park Ridge, Ill., 1968.

9. Barges, A. *The Effect of Capital Structure on the Cost of Capital.* Englewood Cliffs, N.J.: Prentice-Hall, 1963.

10. Barker, C. A. "Price Changes of Stock Dividend Shares at Ex-Dividend Dates." *Journal of Finance* 14 (September 1959): 373–378.

11. Baumol, W. J., Malkiel, B. G., and Quandt, R. E. "The Valuation of Convertible Securities." *Quarterly Journal of Economics* 80 (February 1966): 48–59.

12. Beckman, W. D. "The Effects of Privileged Subscriptions on the Value of the Stock." Paper destroyed but cited in A. S. Dewing, *The Financial Policy of Corporations,* 5th edition (New York: Ronald Press, 1953).

13. Bellemore, D. H., and Blucher, L. N. "A Study of Stock Splits in the Postwar Years." *Financial Analysts Journal* 15 (November 1959): 19–26.

14. Benishay, H. "Variability in Earnings — Price Ratios of Corporate Equities." *American Economic Review* 51 (March 1961): 81–94.

15. Black, F. "Lifetime Investment Strategies for Individuals." Paper prepared for the Seminar on the Analysis of Security Prices, University of Chicago, November 1969.

16. Block, S. B. "The Effect of Mergers and Acquisitions on the Market Value of Common Stock." Ph.D. thesis, Louisiana State University, 1968.

17. Bodenhammer, L. "The Effect of the Size of Public Offerings of Common Stocks upon Pre-Offering Stock Prices." Ph.D. thesis, Harvard Business School, 1968.

18. Boness, A. J. "Elements of a Theory of Stock Option Value." *Journal of Political Economy* 72 (April 1964): 163–175.

19.————. "Some Evidence on the Profitability of Trading in Put and Call Options." In *The Random Character of Stock Market Prices,* edited by P. H. Cootner (Cambridge, Mass.: M.I.T. Press, 1964), pp. 475–496.

20. Bower, R. S., and Bower, D. H. "Risk and the Valuation of Common Stock." *Journal of Political Economy* 77 (May–June 1969): 349–362.

21. Bown, C. C. "Convertible Bonds and the Cost of Capital: Some Theoretical Considerations and Empirical Findings." D.B.A. thesis, University of Washington, 1966.

22. Bradley, J. F. *Fundamentals of Corporation Finance*. Revised edition. New York: Holt, Rinehart & Winston, 1959.

23. Bray, J. N. "The Risk and Use of Debt Financing." Ph.D. thesis, University of California, Los Angeles, 1967.

24. Brealey, R. A. "The Distribution and Independence of Successive Rates of Return in the U.K. Equity Market." *Journal of Business Finance* 2 (Summer 1970): 29–40.

25. Brigham, E. F. "An Analysis of Convertible Debentures: Theory and Some Empirical Evidence." *Journal of Finance* 21 (March 1966): 35–54.

26. Brigham, E. F., and Gordon, M. J. "Leverage, Dividend Policy, and the Cost of Capital." *Journal of Finance* 23 (March 1968): 85–103.

27. Brittain, J. A. *Corporate Dividend Policy*. Washington, D.C.: Brookings Institution, 1966.

28. Bruner, D. M. *Short Selling the U.S.A.* Philadelphia: John C. Winston, 1933.

29. Butters, J. K., Thompson, L. E., and Bollinger, L. L. *Effects of Taxation, Investments by Individuals*. Cambridge, Mass.: Harvard Business School, Division of Research, 1953.

30. Campbell, J. A. and Beranek, W. "Stock Price Behavior on Ex-Dividend Dates." *Journal of Finance* 10 (December 1955): 425–429.

31. Cheney, H. L. "How Good Are Investment Advisory Services?" *Financial Executive* 37 (November 1969): 30–35.

32. Cohen, K. J., and Reid, S. R. "The Benefits and Costs of Bank Mergers." *Journal of Financial and Quantitative Analysis* 1 (December 1966): 15–57.

33. Colker, S. S. "An Analysis of Security Recommendations by

Brokerage Houses." *Quarterly Review of Economics and Business* 3 (Summer 1963): 19–28.

34. Cox, E. B. *Trends in the Distribution of Stock Ownership.* Philadelphia: University of Pennsylvania Press, 1963.

35. Cragg, J., and Malkiel, B. G. "Expectations and the Structure of Share Prices: An Empirical Study." Unpublished paper, 1967.

36. Crum, W. L. "Analysis of Stock Ownership." *Harvard Business Review* 31 (May–June 1953): 36–54.

37. Darling, P. G. "The Influence of Expectations and Liquidity on Dividend Policy." *Journal of Political Economy* 65 (June 1957): 209–224.

38. ———. "A Surrogative Measure of Business Confidence and Its Relation to Stock Prices." *Journal of Finance* 10 (December 1955): 442–458.

39. Davis, J. V. "The Adjustment of Stock Prices to New Information." Ph.D. thesis, Cornell University, 1967.

40. Diamond, J. J. "Earnings Distribution and the Evaluation of Shares: Some Recent Evidence." *Journal of Financial and Quantitative Analysis* 2 (March 1967): 14–29.

41. Donaldson, G. *Corporate Debt Capacity: A Study of Corporate Debt Policy and the Determination of Corporate Debt Capacity.* Cambridge, Mass.: Harvard Business School, Division of Research, 1961.

42. Driscoll, T. E. "Some Aspects of Corporate Insider Stock Holdings and Trading under Section 16(b) of the Securities Exchange Act." M.B.A. thesis, University of Pennsylvania, 1956.

43. Durand, D., and May, A. M. "The Ex-Dividend Behavior of American Telephone and Telegraph Stock." *Journal of Finance* 15 (March 1960): 19–31.

44. Duvel, D. "A Dynamic Programming Model for the Evaluation of Convertible Bonds." Paper prepared for the Seminar on the Analysis of Security Prices, University of Chicago, May 1968.

45. Elton, E. J., and Gruber, M. J. "Marginal Stockholder Tax Rates and the Clientele Effect." *Review of Economics and Statistics* 52 (February 1970): 68–74.

46. Fama, E. F. "Efficient Capital Markets: A Review of Theory and Empirical Work." *Journal of Finance* 25 (May 1970): 383–417.

47. Fama, E. F., and Babiak, H. "Dividend Policy: An Empirical

Analysis." *Journal of the American Statistical Association* 63 (December 1968): 1132–1161.

48. Fama, E. F., Fisher, L., Jensen, M. C., and Roll, R. "The Adjustment of Stock Prices to New Information." *International Economic Review* 10 (February 1969): 1–21.

49. Feldstein, M. S. "Corporate Taxation and Dividend Behavior." *Review of Economic Studies* 37 (January 1970): 57–72.

50. Ferber, R. "Short-Run Effects of Stock Market Services on Stock Prices." *Journal of Finance* 13 (March 1958): 80–95.

51. Fisher, L., and Lorie, J. H. "Rates of Return on Investments in Common Stock: The Year-by-Year Record, 1926–1965." *Journal of Business* 41 (July 1968): 291–316.

52. Frederick, J. G. *The Real Truth about Short Selling*. New York: Business Bourse, 1932.

53. Friend, I. "The Effect of Mutual Funds on Market Performance." Paper prepared for the Seminar on the Analysis of Security Prices, University of Chicago, May 1968.

54. Friend. I., and Herman, E. F. "The SEC through a Glass Darkly." *Journal of Business* 37 (October 1964): 382–403.

55. Friend, I., and Puckett, M. "Dividends and Stock Prices." *American Economic Review* 54 (September 1964): 656–682.

56. Furst, R. W. "Does Listing Increase the Market Price of Common Stocks?" *Journal of Business* 43 (April 1970): 174–180.

57. Ganz, L. J. "An Empirical Examination of the Relation between Capital Structure and Business Risk." Ph.D. thesis, New York University, 1968.

58. Glass, G. A. "Extensive Insider Accumulation as an Indicator of Near-Term Stock Price Performance." Ph.D. thesis, Ohio State University, 1966.

59. Godfrey, M. D., Granger, C. W. J., and Morgenstern, O. "The Random Walk Hypothesis of Stock Market Behavior." *Kyklos* 17 (1964): 1–30.

60. Gordon, M. J. "Dividends, Earnings and Stock Prices." *Review of Economics and Statistics* 41 (May 1959): 99–105.

61. Gort, M., and Hogarty, T. F. "New Evidence on Mergers." *Journal of Law and Economics* 13 (April 1970): 167–184.

62. Graham, B., and Dodd, D. L. *Security Analysis*. 3rd edition. New York: McGraw-Hill, 1951.

63. Granger, C. W. J., and Morgenstern, O. "Spectral Analysis of New York Stock Market Prices." *Kyklos* 16 (1963): 1–27.

64. Granville, J. E. *A Strategy of Daily Stock Market Timing for Maximum Profit*. Englewood Cliffs, N.J.: Prentice-Hall, 1960.

65. Hamada, R. S. "An Analysis of Diffusion Indices of Insiders' Transactions." S. M. thesis, Massachusetts Institute of Technology, 1961.

66. Hanna, M. "Short Interest: Bullish or Bearish? — Comment." *Journal of Finance* 23 (June 1968): 520–523.

67. Hardy, C. O. *Odd Lot Trading on the New York Stock Exchange*. Washington, D.C.: Brookings Institution, 1939.

68. Hogarty, T. F. "The Profitability of Corporate Mergers." *Journal of Business* 43 (July 1970): 317–327.

69. Horowitz, I. "A Rating of Mutual Fund Managements' Investment Ability." *Industrial Management Review* 7 (Fall 1965): 65–76.

70. Jensen, M. C. "The Performance of Mutual Funds in the Period 1945–1964." *Journal of Finance* 23 (May 1968): 389–416.

71. Johnson, H. W., and Simon, J. L. "The Success of Mergers: The Case of Advertising Agencies." *Bulletin of the Oxford University Institute of Economics and Statistics* 31 (1969): 139–144.

72. Jolivet, V. "The Weighted Average Marginal Tax Rate on Dividends Received by Individuals in the U.S." *American Economic Review* 56 (June 1966): 473–477.

73. Kaish, S. "Odd Lot Profit and Loss Performance." *Financial Analysts Journal* 25 (September–October 1969): 83–92.

74. Kartchner, E. C. "A Distributed Lag Analysis of the Dividends Earnings Relationship of Some Listed, Non-Financial U.S. Corporations." Ph.D. thesis, University of Washington, 1966.

75. Kassouf, S. T. *The Evaluation of Convertible Securities*. New York: Analytical Investors, 1966.

76. ———. "Stock Price Random Walks: Some Supporting Evidence." *Review of Economics and Statistics* 50 (May 1968): 275–278.

77. ———. "A Theory and an Econometric Model for Common Stock Purchase Warrants." Ph.D. thesis, Columbia University, 1965.

78. Katz, R. C. "The Profitability of Put and Call Option Writing." *Industrial Management Review* 5 (Fall 1963): 55–69.

79. Kelly, E. M. "The Profitability of Growth through Mergers." Ph.D. thesis, Columbia University, 1965.

80. Kewley, T. J., and Stevenson, R. A. "The Odd-Lot Theory as Revealed by Purchase and Sales Statistics for Individual Stocks." *Financial Analysts Journal* 23 (September–October 1967): 103–106.

81. ———. "The Odd-Lot Theory for Individual Stocks: A Reply." *Financial Analysts Journal* 25 (January–February 1969): 99–104.

82. Kisor, M., Jr., and Messner, V. A. "The Filter Approach and Earnings Forecasts." *Financial Analysts Journal* 25 (January–February 1969): 109–116.

83. Kisor, M., Jr., and Niederhoffer, V. "Odd-Lot Short Sales Ratio: It Signals a Market Rise." *Barron's*, September 1, 1969, p. 8.

84. Klein, D. J. "The Odd-Lot Stock Trading Theory." Ph.D. thesis, Michigan State University, 1964.

85. Kruizenga, R. J. "Put and Call Options: A Theoretical and Market Analysis." Ph.D. thesis, Massachusetts Institute of Technology, 1956.

86. Kuehner, C. D. "Underwritten Common Stock Offers, 1955–1964: Considerations and a Descriptive Under-Pricing Model." Ph.D. thesis, New York University, 1966.

87. Leffler, G. L. "Stock Rights." *Barron's*, September 16, 1957, pp. 15 ff.

88. Lehr, M. E., and Newbould, G. D. "New Issues — Activity and Pricing Performance 1964–1967." *Investment Analyst* 18 (October 1967): 20–23.

89. Lintner, J. "Distribution of Incomes of Corporations among Dividends, Retained Earnings and Taxes." *American Economic Review* 46 (May 1956): 97–113.

90. ———. "Optimal Dividends and Corporate Growth under Uncertainty." *Quarterly Journal of Economics* 78 (February 1964): 68–71.

91. Loomis, C. J. "A Case for Dropping Dividends." *Fortune,* June 15, 1968, pp. 181 ff.

92. Lorie, J. H., and Halpern, P. "Conglomerates: The Rhetoric and the Evidence." *Journal of Law and Economics* 13 (April 1970): 149–166.

93. Lorie, J. H., and Niederhoffer, V. "Predictive and Statistical

Properties of Insider Trading." Paper prepared for the Seminar on the Analysis of Security Prices, University of Chicago, May 1967. Published in the *Journal of Law and Economics* 11 (April 1968): 35–53.

94. McCarthy, G. D. *Acquisitions and Mergers.* New York: Ronald Press, 1963.

95. Malkiel, B. G., and Quandt, R. E. *Strategies and Rational Decisions in the Securities Option Market.* Cambridge, Mass.: M.I.T. Press, 1969.

96. Mayor, T. H. "Short Trading Activities and the Price of Equities: Some Simulation and Regression Results." *Journal of Financial and Quantitative Analysis* 3 (September 1968): 283–298.

97. Merjos, A. "Going on the Big Board." *Barron's,* May 1, 1967, pp. 9–10.

98. ———. "Going on the Big Board: Stocks Act Better before Listing than Right Afterward." *Barron's,* January 29, 1962, pp. 54 ff.

99. ———. "Like Money in the Bank: Big Board Listing, the Record Suggests, Is a Valuable Asset." *Barron's,* July 8, 1963, pp. 94 ff.

100. ———. "Lunch at the Analysts." *Barron's,* October 9, 1961, pp. 5 ff.

101. Merrett, A. J., Howe, M., and Newbould, G. D. *Equity Issues and the London Capital Market.* London: Longmans, Green, 1967.

102. Miller, M. H., and Modigliani, F. "Dividend Policy, Growth, and the Valuation of Shares." *Journal of Business* 34 (October 1961): 411–433.

103. ———. "Some Estimates of the Cost of Capital to the Electric Utility Industry, 1954–1957." *American Economic Review* 56 (June 1966): 333–391.

104. Mock, E. J. "An Evaluation of Borrower Risk in Industrial Companies Employing Convertible Subordinated Debentures." Ph.D. thesis, Ohio State University, 1964.

105. Modigliani, F., and Miller, M. H. "Corporate Income Taxes and the Cost of Capital: A Correction." *American Economic Review* 53 (June 1963): 433–443.

106. ———. "The Cost of Capital, Corporation Finance and the Theory of Investment." *American Economic Review* 48 (June 1958): 261–297.

107. Murphy, J. E., Jr. "Return, Payout and Growth." *Financial Analysts Journal* 23 (May–June 1967): 91–96.

108. Nelson, R. L. *Merger Movements in American Industry 1895–1956.* Princeton, N.J.: Princeton University Press, 1959.

109. Niederhoffer, V. "World Events and Stock Prices: A Study of Large *New York Times* Headlines and Subsequent Movements in the Standard & Poor's Composite Index." PhD. thesis, University of Chicago, 1969.

110. Oliver, R. B. "Cash Tender Offers." M.B.A. thesis, New York University, 1969.

111. Osborne, M. F. M. "Periodic Structure in the Brownian Motion of Stock Prices." *Operations Research* 10 (May–June 1962): 345–379.

112. Over-the-Counter Information Bureau. *Considerations in Listing on a Stock Exchange.* New York: Arthur Schmidt & Associates, 1965.

113. Pilcher, J. C. *Raising Capital with Convertible Securities.* Ann Arbor: University of Michigan, 1955.

114. Poensgen, O. H. "The Valuation of Convertible Bonds, Part I." *Industrial Management Review* 7 (Fall 1965): 77–92.

115. ———. "The Valuation of Convertible Bonds, Part II." *Industrial Management Review* 7 (Spring 1966): 83–98.

116. Pratt, S. P. "Relationship between Risk and Rate of Return for Common Stocks." D.B.A. thesis, Indiana University, 1966.

117. Pratt, S. P., and DeVere, C. W. "Relationship between Insider Trading and Rates of Return for NYSE Common Stocks, 1960–1966." Paper prepared for the Seminar on the Analysis of Security Prices, University of Chicago, May 1968.

118. Readett, P. B., Jr. "The Price Behavior of Stocks on Their Ex-Dividend Dates." S.M. thesis, Massachusetts Institute of Technology, 1956.

119. Reid, S. R. *Mergers, Managers, and the Economy.* New York: McGraw-Hill, 1968.

120. Reilly, F. K., and Hatfield, K. "Experience with New Stock Issues." *Financial Analysts Journal* 25 (September–October 1969): 73–82.

121. Robinson, F. A., Jr. "An Inquiry into the Dividend Practices of Industrial Corporations." Ph.D. thesis, New York University, 1951.

122. Rogoff, D. L. "The Forecasting Properties of Insiders' Transactions." D.B.A. thesis, Michigan State University, 1964.

123. Rosen, M.N. "Strategies for Writers of Puts and Calls." S.M. thesis, Massachusetts Institute of Technology, 1965.

124. Rosett, R. "Estimating the Utility of Wealth from Call Option Transactions." In *Risk Aversion and Portfolio Choice*, edited by D. D. Hester and J. Tobin. New York: John Wiley and Sons, 1967.

125. Rubner, A. *The Ensnared Shareholder*. London: Macmillan, 1965.

126. Ruff, R. T. "The Effect of Selection and Recommendation of a Stock of the Month." *Financial Analysts Journal* 19 (March–April 1963): 41–43.

127. Samuelson, P. A. "Rational Theory of Warrant Pricing." *Industrial Management Review* 6 (Spring 1965): 13–31.

128. Sarachman, E. T. "A Study of Rights Offerings on the New York Stock Exchange from 1950 to 1961." M.B.A. thesis, New York University, 1963.

129. Scholes, M. "A Test of the Competitive Market Hypothesis: The Market for New Issues and Secondary Offerings." Ph.D. thesis, University of Chicago, 1969.

130. Securities and Exchange Commission. *Report of the Special Study of the Securities Markets*. Washington, D.C.: Government Printing Office, 1963.

131. ———. *Report on Put and Call Options*. Washington, D.C.: Government Printing Office, 1961.

132. Segall, J. "Merging for Fun and Profit." *Industrial Management Review* 9 (Winter 1968): 17–30.

133. Seneca, J. J. "Short Interest: Bearish or Bullish?" *Journal of Finance* 22 (March 1967): 67–70.

134. ———. "Short Interest: Bullish or Bearish? — Reply." *Journal of Finance* 23 (June 1968): 524–527.

135. Sharpe, W. F. "Mutual Fund Performance." *Journal of Business* 39 (January 1966): 119–138.

136. Shelton, J. P. "The Relation of the Price of a Warrant to the Price of Its Associated Stock — Part I." *Financial Analysts Journal* 23 (May–June 1967): 143–151.

137. ————. "The Relation of the Price of a Warrant to the Price of Its Associated Stock — Part II." *Financial Analysts Journal* 23 (July–August 1967): 88–99.

138. Smith, R. "Cost of Capital in the Oil Industry." Hectograph. Pittsburgh: Carnegie Institute of Technology, 1955.

139. Smith, R. D. "Short Interest and Stock Market Prices." *Financial Analysts Journal* 24 (December 1968): 151–154.

140. Soldofsky, R. M., and Johnson, C. R. "Rights Timing." *Financial Analysts Journal* 23 (July–August 1967): 101–104.

141. Sprenkle, C. M. "Warrant Prices as Indicators of Expectations and Preferences." *Yale Economic Essays* 1 (Fall 1961): 179–231.

142. Stigler, G. J. "Public Regulation of the Securities Markets." *Journal of Business* 37 (April 1964): 117–142.

143. Stoffels, J. D. "Stock Recommendations by Investment Advisory Services: Immediate Effects on Market Pricing." *Financial Analysts Journal* 22 (March 1966): 77–86.

144. Stoll, H. R. "The Relationship between Put and Call Option Prices." *Journal of Finance* 24 (December 1969): 801–824.

145. Stoll, H. R., and Curley, A. J. "Small Business and the New Issues Market for Equities." *Journal of Financial and Quantitative Analysis* 5 (September 1970): 309–322.

146. Synnott, T. W., III. "Time Series Analysis for Investment Decisions." Paper prepared for the Seminar on the Analysis of Security Prices, University of Chicago, November 1968.

147. "That Post-Listing Tired Feeling." *Forbes,* November 1, 1964, p. 16.

148. Thompson, G. C. and Walsh, F. J., Jr. "Companies Stress Dividend Consistency." *National Industrial Conference Board Management Record* 25 (January 1963): 30–36.

149. Thorp, E. O., and Kassouf, S. *Beat the Market.* New York: Random House, 1967.

150. Van Horne, J. C. "New Listings and Their Price Behavior." *Journal of Finance* 25 (September 1970): 783–794.

151. ————. "Warrant Valuation in Relation to Volatility and Opportunity Costs." *Industrial Management Review* 10 (Spring 1969): 19–32.

152. Walter, J. E. *Dividend Policy and Enterprise Valuation.* Belmont, Calif.: Wadsworth Publishing Company, 1967.

153. Waud, R. N. "Public Interpretation of Discount Rate Changes: Evidence on the 'Announcement' Effect." *Econometrica* 38 (March 1970): 231–250.

154. Weil, R. L., Segall, J. E. and Green, D., Jr. "Premiums on Convertible Bonds." *Journal of Finance* 23 (June 1968): 445–463.

155. Weller, K. J. "An Analysis and Appraisal of Rights Offerings as a Method of Raising Equity Capital." Ph.D. thesis, University of Michigan, 1961.

156. Weston, J. F., and Brigham, E. F. *Managerial Finance.* 2nd edition. New York: Holt, Rinehart & Winston, 1966.

157. Whitbeck, V., and Kisor, M. "A New Tool in Investment Decision Making." *Financial Analysts Journal* 19 (May–June 1963): 55–62.

158. Williams, D. E. "Profitability of Writing 6-Month 10-Day Calls." M.B.A. thesis, New York University, 1967.

159. Wippern, R. F. "Financial Structure and the Value of the Firm." *Journal of Finance* 21 (December 1966): 615–634.

160. Wu, Hsiu-Kwang. "Corporate Insider Trading, Profitability and Stock Price Movement." Ph.D. thesis, University of Pennsylvania, 1963.

161. Ying, C. C. "Stock Market Prices and Volume of Sales." *Econometrica* 34 (July 1966): 676–685.

Index

Note: Page numbers following names of authors refer to pages on which works cited in the References are discussed.